Professor Harvey Wasserman... York City, graduating from Queens College of ... with a Bachelor of Science degree in Chemistry. He completed his psychiatric training at the Menninger Foundation, Topeka, Kansas, where he was awarded a Fellowship in Psychiatry and served as Lecturer in Psychiatry at Kansas University College of Medicine. In addition to 36 years in the private practice of psychiatry, he served as Assistant Clinical Professor of Psychiatry, Yale University College of Medicine form 1966 to 1981. At Yale he was Director of Education and Training at one of the Medical School Teaching and Research Hospitals. He has given lectures and workshops around the world. He has studied many forms of psychotherapy and healing, from bioenergetic analysis to traditional Chinese Medicine. He has had extensive anthropological contact with tribal peoples and native healers all over the world. He currently lives in the Burren in County Clare and practices psychotherapy in Galway.

THE HEALING ROAD

HARVEY WASSERMAN

AUBURN HOUSE

To my teachers, who taught me.
To my patients, who taught me.

Published in 1995 by
Auburn House,
A division of Salmon Publishing Ltd,
Upper Fairhill, Galway

© Harvey Wasserman 1995

Reprinted 1995

The moral right of the author has been asserted.

A catalogue record for this book is available from the British Library.

ISBN 1 897648 36 7

Cover painting by Harvey Wasserman
Cover design by Poolbeg Group Services Ltd
Set by Poolbeg Group Services Ltd in Garamond 10.25/13
Printed by The Guernsey Press Co Ltd, Vale, Guernsey, Channel Islands.

CONTENTS

INTRODUCTION

Introducing myself to you is a special experience. Perhaps we shall never meet; perhaps we *shall* meet. in either case I am sitting at my desk writing to introduce myself and something about this book. The desk at which I write looks out at the most remarkable scene – the Burren – an Irish wilderness, its glacially carved limestone hills illuminated in the setting sun. The sun somehow etches the sculptural quality of the eroded stone, of the terraced stone, carved into hills by glaciers 10,000 years ago. A herd of multi-coloured, shaggy-haired, long-horned, wild mountain goats feed briskly in the distance. The Burren is a miracle of geology, a miracle of botany, a miracle of archaeology. The writing of this book is a small miracle, and a small Irish miracle at that.

In December of 1992 I retired from 37 years in the practice of psychiatry. Attracted by the uniqueness of the Burren – particularly its mysterious, almost mystical energy – I decided to start a new life in this 100 square miles that strangely called to me. Ireland surrounds the Burren, but was an added, largely unknown attraction.

I had not missed working with patients for over a year after my move to County Clare and the Burren. This surprised me after 37 years of preoccupation in a discipline that I loved. Unexpectedly I was given the opportunity of briefly working psychotherapeutically with two young people. Much to my surprise, not only hadn't I forgotten everything I had been doing for the past 37 years, but I actually enjoyed the experience of working with them.

Perhaps it would be fun and challenging to set up a small, part-time private practice in Ireland – starting all over again, doing only the kinds of therapeutic work that I particularly enjoyed – and instead of being a retiree, becoming a part of the community.

I spoke to Nuala Eising, Director of the Burren School of Homoeopathy, who said, "Your credentials won't mean anything here in Ireland; the Irish will want to see you, to get a personal impression of you, if you ever hope to have any patients come to your office."

That night I went to sleep, and awoke from a vivid dream with the subjects for five lectures in my mind. I leaped out of bed and quickly wrote them down before I forgot. The subjects were: The Nature of Love, The Deterioration and Healing of a Loving Relationship, Fear and Anxiety, Depression, and last, Getting Stuck on Your Life's Journey, including Spiritual Aspects of Mental Health.

I rented a small hotel meeting space that could accommodate 100 people for five sequential Wednesday evenings, to match my five lecture subjects. I placed a small ad in the local paper, and was fortunate enough to have a very laudatory interview printed in the Galway Advertiser by Jeff O'Connell.

The night of the first lecture arrived. I came to the lecture hall early to make sure that all the facilities were in place, and noticed that about 1/3 of the seats were filled. Even in my short stay in Ireland, I had learned that the Irish never come to anything early, so this was a little surprising.

By ten minutes before I was due to begin my lecture, the room was entirely filled, every seat and every place anyone could stand. By the time my lecture was to start, a distressed assistant manager came and said, "There are people everywhere. They're crowding the halls. They're crowding the stairwells. They're crowding the lobby. They don't want to go away. When I tell them there's no room, they want to talk to you. What can I do? There are fire laws. There are insurance problems."

I went to talk to the people waiting outside, who pleaded with me (some angrily) that many of them had come long distances to attend my lecture – how could I turn them away? I didn't know what I was going to do, when suddenly the assistant manager realized that the grand ballroom of the hotel was not engaged that evening, and we could move my presentation there.

We managed to get close to 400 people into the ballroom. Hundreds more we know we turned away, and possibly still additional hundreds, seeing the large crowds, turned themselves away from the meeting site.

The first lecture went very well. At tea with the assistant manager after it was over, she said, "No one left. That means you're going to have even a larger attendance next week." But alas, the large ballroom was no longer available. I managed to secure the use of the O'Flaherty Theatre at University College Galway, which seats 370 people. To my complete astonishment, not only were these seats filled, but every place on the stairs and at the side of the podium was jammed with eager attendees, and unknown numbers of people were turned away.

I was stunned. I would have been happy if 40 people had shown up the first night. Why were all these people coming?

Just then I received a call from the office of Gay Byrne. Alice O'Sullivan, a staff member on the radio show, had heard about me. My lecture about love fit perfectly into their plans for the coming Valentine's Week series of programs.

I went to Dublin. I was told that I would be interviewed for 15 or 20 minutes. I *thought* it had been only 15 or maybe 20 minutes, or perhaps a little longer, when Gay let me know that the interview was over and I staggered outside, amazed to discover that I had been on the air (with some interruptions for news, etc.) for an hour and ten minutes.

If I hadn't felt it before, I now felt that I had gone for a simple ride in a small boat on a placid lake, and suddenly found myself in the ocean, propelled by a giant tidal wave. The crowds that came to my lectures were beyond counting. It was necessary because of fire laws to station guards at the door and hand out tickets. I received about 400 letters that took me months to answer.

And to me most miraculous of all, several publishers contacted me and wished to publish my lectures.

On a Sunday morning that I'll never forget, I was sleeping late and lazily when my phone rang. A woman's voice apologized for calling me and asking me something rather strange. "My name is Jessie Lendennie. I publish poetry," she said. "I've been attending your lectures, and something in your use of language made me think that you write poetry. Do you write poetry?"

"I have a suitcase full," I replied, as my knees gave out from under me and I collapsed onto a nearby couch. I hardly told anyone in the United States that I wrote poetry. At best they'd be uninterested; at worst they'd be derogatory.

Within two days I had shown Jessie my poetry, and to her and my astonishment, it was exactly the kind of poetry that she was looking for, to start a new publishing company, Auburn House, in the West of Ireland. Jessie became the publisher of *The Healing Road* and its accompanying volume of poetry and commentaries, *At the Centre of Time*.

I have had many requests to lecture all over Ireland. And suddenly, the unknown country that surrounded the Burren reached out to me, became friendly, began to educate me about itself. It was as if Atlantis had reemerged from the ocean.

My lecture series continued to be overwhelmingly subscribed, with incessant demands for tapes and books. In stunned wondering, I searched my mind to understand this amazing occurrence. Ireland is a changing country, reaching out for new ways of being and organizing and thinking in the world. Perhaps that was part of it. People told me that I didn't talk like an American, I didn't use big words.

4

Especially, I didn't talk down to them. "You make sense," they said. All of this explained, but didn't seem enough to account for everything that happened.

This book is the result of those lectures. I have taken the information in the lectures and added to and amplified the content of my talks. In a book I am not limited by time constraints, or chairs in a lecture hall that cannot move.

I hope you will find this book of mine a very rich meal. The information in it is very condensed, the exercises numerous, some unusual. It is my hope that your joining me in this book is an intense experience that will engage you in ways that are obvious and in ways that are subtle, in changing your consciousness and moving you forward on *your* journey, on your healing road.

You may find that you can only read this book in short segments. Let your experience judge that for you. You may find that you want to skim the book to get an overall feeling before you chew on its contents. Even so, you still may find that small bites seem to fill your appetite. Do not be surprised if, as I hope, you have a very enjoyable experience playing in these fields of my imagination and experience. If you have trouble remembering much of what has been written, there will be plenty of opportunities to go back again and review. I hope you will find the exercises interesting and useful. My guess is that you will not attempt all of them. Those that you do experiment with will certainly lead you to one or two that you find particularly useful. Remember that one useful experience is not enough to change years of repetitive behavior. The legendary Sheherezade told stories for 40 days and 40 nights. It takes about that time – about 5 or six weeks – of repetitive healing experience before you have incorporated and earned your new learning. If only one or two of the ideas, if only one or two of the exercises in this work have opened your mind, have changed your experience and have helped to eliminate any 'stuckness' in your life, then all the joyous effort that has gone into preparing this work will have been worthwhile.

CHAPTER ONE

The Nature of Love

Love is the centre of life. With it you can have a good life. Without it you will have an empty life. If you have everything in life but love, you have nothing. The best example of this that I am aware of was a very wealthy gentleman, J. Paul Getty. I never met him, but I saw an interview with him on television. J. Paul Getty had more wealth than most of us can imagine. He came from a family of great wealth and he multiplied that wealth many times. He knew how to accumulate wealth. My impression of him over the television was that he was a miserable, chronically depressed man, depressed but functional. To my best knowledge, he had no love in his life. No sensible sane person would have accepted the quality of his existence for all his wealth. Some time before the video program that I saw, one of his grandchildren, a grandson, asked for money from his grandfather. His grandfather said no. The grandson then staged a mock kidnapping and to intimidate his grandfather into sending money,went as far as to cut off his own ear and mail it to his grandfather as a threat of further mutilation by the kidnappers. The grandfather said no.

If you have love, but only a little of the material part of life, there is a possibility that you can have a good life.

What is love? Love is usually defined as an emotion. Like fear. Like anger. But we intuitively know that love is more than that. Love is a divine, cosmic energy which integrates with our individual vital life force and expresses itself as an emotion.

Love is a divine, cosmic energy which integrates with our individual vital life force and expresses itself as an emotion.

Place this definition of love in a corner of your mind. There will be more about this later.

There are many aspects to love. We all know that we Irish are reticent at public displays of emotion and affection. Despite that, pick a partner. You can do this privately, or more publicly if you can tolerate the public display. I am going to instruct you in how to give and receive a very special hug.

It's best for the purpose of this exercise to pick as a partner someone you are comfortable with, and someone of the same height. Put your arms around each other, but only let your chests gently touch, holding your hands at the centre of the back, along the spine, just opposite the area where your chests are touching, approximately at heart level. Make sure that your knees are slightly, gently bent, and that your eyes are closed. Pay attention to your breathing. Keep it slow and deep.

What is your experience like? Do you feel a melting, as if your body was turning to liquid, a liquid flow of love cascading gently down into the earth? Along with this melting experience, was there any difficulty in tolerating the hug? Did you have to terminate it rapidly? Were you comfortable, or was there anxiety? Most people are unable to tolerate this hug for more than a few seconds. Very different from other kinds of hugs. Very different from a bear hug. It is not unusual for feelings of discomfort and anxiety to make it necessary to terminate the hug even after the most pleasurable experience of mutual melting. Further on in this chapter you will understand why there is discomfort after the pleasure and some ways to heal this anxiety.

Love is scary. It makes us vulnerable. Vulnerable to what?

7

To pain. It melts our egos into nothingness, like Little Black Sambo's tigers melting into butter, so we stand naked and unprotected.

A. Self Love

Self esteem is a major facet of love. If love is the centre of life, self love, self esteem, is the foundation of life. Out loud, say to yourself or to someone you feel comfortable with, looking them softly in the eye and using their name, "I love myself." And rate it one to ten, one meaning that it is totally untrue, and ten meaning it is absolutely true. You need a consistent seven and eight to have a good quality of life. There is no quality to life without self esteem.

Self love, self esteem, provides us with protection against the pain and vulnerability of love. If you had 100 percent self love, you would never experience pain. You would see others' behavior, even if directed against you, as *their* problem. You would feel sad, but you would know it had nothing to do with yourself. Unfortunately, maybe 50 or 75 people every century reach the level of 100 percent self esteem.

As possible evidence that self esteem protects you against pain, perhaps you can recall a painful childhood event that you know now as an adult would no longer hurt you. As there is increased learning and increased self esteem, events that were previously painful no longer hurt us emotionally. We know we do not deserve the assault on our love. We know that it doesn't have anything to do with us. Instead of feeling emotional pain, we see the behavior of the other person. You may be curious about that behavior. You may feel sad that they felt it necessary to behave in such a destructive way. But there no longer is any pain. As your learning and self esteem grow, closer and closer to an ultimate 100 percent, eventually no one could hurt you. No one could inflict emotional pain. Remember that emotional pain is damage that we allow to the parts of us that love.

Self esteem and its cousin, self respect, are not to be confused with self-centreedness, egotism or arrogance. Self esteem is how you feel about yourself, the amount of love and caring that you feel for yourself. Self respect is a variant, an aspect of self esteem but related to how you see yourself, as equal or unequal to other people around you. Self-centreedness has nothing to do with self love, but has to do with paying attention only to one's own interests and values, with no attention to anyone else other than the self. Arrogance is the illusion that one is superior to those around you. With self love, there is clear vision about yourself, clear vision about who you are, clear vision about your relationship and valuing of others. So with self esteem and self love, there is no necessity for self-centredness, egotism or arrogance. Humbleness is the loving acceptance of who you are and your place in the scheme of things. Self esteem, far from taking away our ability to love others, as self-centredness, egotism and arrogance do, makes loving others easier, pleasanter, simpler. Egotism, self-centredness and arrogance are false masks, false self esteem covering discomfort and insecurity.

Self love originally comes from the amount, the percentage, of unconditional love you received as a child. It's very rare for any of us to be so fortunate as to get 100 percent unconditional love, love without any expectations, without any questions, without conditions of any kind. One of the great values of grandmothers and grandfathers is that more often they can give us the pure love that we call unconditional love, and become very valuable teachers of our loving of ourselves. If we have such unconditional love, even if we are fortunate only to have it for four or five or six years, it can make a major positive impact on the whole course of our lives.

A very simple exercise can give you the feeling and experience of unconditional love. Please refer to the diagram showing the location of the chakras. [diagram A]

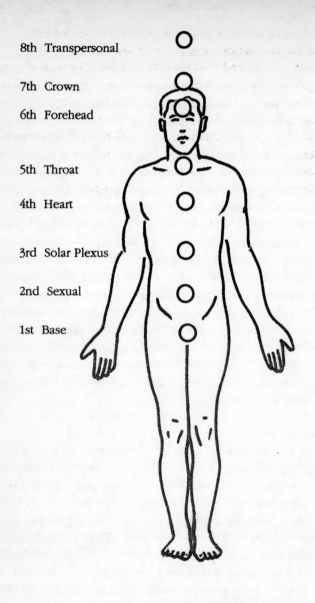

8th Transpersonal

7th Crown

6th Forehead

5th Throat

4th Heart

3rd Solar Plexus

2nd Sexual

1st Base

THE EIGHT MAJOR CHAKRAS

The chakras are a Hindu system of energy centres found along the midline of the soft side of the body.

Move your hand from below to above the chakra, in a very slow, sweeping movement, as if you were stroking velvet. Say to yourself over each chakra, in the following order: fourth chakra, fifth chakra, third chakra, sixth chakra, second chakra, seventh chakra, first chakra, and transpersonal chakra . . . saying out loud, using your own name, "Welcome, [NAME]. Welcome, [NAME]." Say it with warmth and tenderness in your voice, and see what that feels like.

If you can, find a partner and share this experience. Have them lie on a bed or on the ground. Ask them in their mind's eye, with their eyes closed, to go back to the feeling that they were very little children. And as you kneel over them, moving your hand from below, across and above the chakra in a slow, sensual manner, with sincerity and tenderness in your voice, repeat at each chakra, "Welcome, Susan. Welcome, Sarah. Welcome, John." [Using your partner's given name] And then reverse the experience. Let them do it to you. And feel even for a brief moment the glorious feeling of being welcomed, lovingly and unconditionally, into this world.

You might want to say before and after this experience, "I was born to love myself," and again value it from one to ten, ten meaning it's absolutely true, one meaning it's not true at all. See if the experience of unconditional love given by yourself, given by a friend, raises the level of self love that you're experiencing.

I once told a patient to repeat the sentence, "I was born to love myself," to which he responded, snappily, "Yes, I was born to love myself, but I was raised to hate myself." To a child, the family is the whole world. When that world, that family, conveys love with conditions, that tells us, the child, that we are not worthy of love, we are not intuitively and naturally in the course of events worthy of love, but we have to earn it. A child always believes what his family, his world, tells him. And the imprint, any imprint, in the rapidly

11

developing brain of a child, is hard to erase, is written in stone. Children love their parents, love their family. The image of themselves created by their world, their family, is clung to throughout life, out of loyalty, often misguided loyalty, to their beloved family.

So it is very hard to change self esteem. It requires a lot of work. It happens slowly. But if you improve the quality of your self esteem, if you increase your self esteem, ten percent, the quality of your life is increased 100 percent. It's a very worthwhile effort.

Another exercise, another unusual one, which can increase self esteem, is done simply by moving your body and breathing properly. Lie on your back, perhaps with a rolled up towel in the small of your back. Before you start the exercise, check the level of your self esteem by saying once again, "I love myself," and valuing it from one to ten.

With your eyes closed, as you breathe in, and your belly fills up with your breathing, rotate your pelvis into the ground. As you breathe out, lift your pelvis off the ground, moving it upwards so each vertebra slowly rolls upwards with the exhalation, until the area slightly above the back of the heart is so moved upward. And then, gently, with the in breath, lower the spine onto the ground, let the belly come out, and once again tip the pelvis into the floor.

It is important in this exercise not to raise the spine as a single unit and jerk your pelvis up off the ground, but to roll it upward.

Once you have mastered the technique of this exercise, lose yourself in the cycle of breathing and movement for about one to two minutes. And then once again check how you feel about yourself. Do you feel better about yourself? Do you feel warm inside? Do you feel softer? Is your voice mellifluous? Is there a melting when you say, "I love myself," so that you know the level has gone up? It's amazing that a simple breathing and body movement exercise can raise your self esteem. So the body and the breath can alter thought and feeling. It's something to think about.

In fact, things can work the other way around. There is a simple exercise to establish this. Ask a willing partner to sit in a chair with his back to you. (Or have the partner do that to you.) If you are right-handed, place your right hand on their shoulder and press down with a moderate, not excessive amount of pressure. Ask your partner in the chair to think positive things about themselves, and after they have done this for a short period of time, ask them to stand up. Have them feel how easy it is, or hard it is, to stand up; how easy it is to resist the pressure of your hand as they stand up.

Then ask them to berate themselves mentally, or out loud if they feel comfortable, say all the negative things they have ever thought about themselves, quietly in their minds or noisily in their minds, or out loud. Then ask them to stand up against the same amount of pressure. Do they feel different? Is the vigor with which they stand up the same? Is their body as coordinated when their thoughts are negative as when they originally stood up when their thoughts were positive?

The chances are that you'll discover that standing up is a very different experience when you are thinking positively about yourself, and you are thinking negatively about yourself. It is amazing to discover very clearly and graphically how much our thinking affects the way our body moves and is coordinated and resists pressure in this world. That also is something to think about. It is why we believe that thinking can change the way our bodies react, that thinking can cause us to feel badly, in fact, to become ill.

It is more unusual to realize that by changing the breath and the body, we can change our attitudes and thinking. More about this later.

Another simple technique which if repeated can have profound effects on the way we feel about ourselves is simply to use a mirror. With that mirror make eye contact with yourself and state positive things about yourself, ones that you know are true, ones that you suspect are true.

Always using the third person, 'you,' never 'I.' You want to experiment between 'you' and 'I.' I think you will find that when you say 'you' to the person in the mirror, that the effect is more powerful. Simply state that "You are intelligent," "You are loving," "You are a good person," "You have a good heart," "You have good values," whatever positive things you have heard about yourself, and you suspect or know are true.

You can do this out loud whenever possible, and if you pass a mirror, when other people would think you are a little strange for talking out loud, you can do it quietly in your head. The most important time to do it is in the morning when you get up to go to the bathroom to empty your bladder. At that moment you are half asleep and half awake, and your unconscious is really hanging out. If you can hesitate for a moment before the bathroom mirror, and stay and do this exercise, "You're a good person, you're intelligent, you're loving," it will have even a more profound effect.

Another way to approach the whole issue of self esteem and its adversary, self negation and self torture, is to take a day in any week and write down all the negative thoughts that you catch yourself thinking. And remember, if you have been doing a lot of self negation, as most of us do, you probably at the beginning only write down one out of every ten disparaging thoughts you think about yourself.

Now if we imagine our mind as a circle, and the negative thoughts as black spots peppering the surface of that circle, we have a pretty good idea of the powerful effect that self negation has on our minds and our feeling about ourselves and the way we behave.

Imagine that there is a part of yourself that is totally responsible for all the negative thoughts that are going through your mind, and give it a name. The name I use is Self Torturer, but it could be Hanging Judge, it could be Father, it could be Mother, it could be George. It could be anything that feels right and is short and pithy.

14

Whenever you catch yourself saying anything negative to yourself about yourself, respond to that thought by simply stating, using your word for that part of yourself, "Hi there, Self Torturer – you're back." Say it in a neutral, slightly friendly way, in a manner very similar to the way you would respond to a neighbour that you were not terribly fond of, but wanted to be polite to, who was on the other side of the street. And you would say, "Hi, Mrs. O'Neill, how are you?" and then go about your way. If the torturing, self negating thought comes back, simply repeat that thought in the same neutral, slightly friendly manner.

What you will find, over a period of time is that the thoughts come back less and less, and when they do come back they are further and further apart. Remember that any time that you struggle against such negative thought, you are putting more energy into it. It strengthens the negativity rather than weakening it.

When any part of yourself that is undesirable, that is poisonous and toxic, feels normal and natural, the word for that is ego syntonic. It feels comfortable. It feels like it belongs. You have been doing this self negation for so long, it seems like a natural part of yourself. You don't even have to think about believing it; it is second nature. What we are trying to do with this simple technique is to make that ego syntonic thinking and attitudes ego dystonic, so that they feel uncomfortable, they feel foreign, they feel that they don't belong. It can almost be visualized as a surgical technique where we're pushing all these thoughts together to one part of the mind so that we can recognize them, feel their disharmony, feel how wrong they are, and then slowly surgically cutting them out of our minds. As they leave our mind and are separated from us, they no longer have any validity and disappear the way soap bubbles burst after a few seconds of floating through the air. *[Diagram B, Separating Negative Thoughts From the Ego]*

Another exercise to promote self esteem – and I recommend that you try all of these exercises and decide which ones feel most useful for you, and then repeat them – also requires a partner.

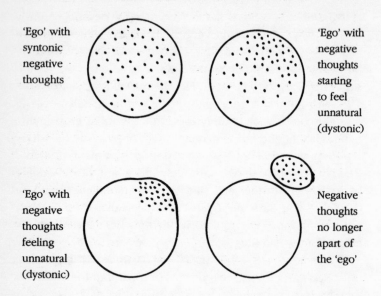

'Ego' with syntonic negative thoughts

'Ego' with negative thoughts starting to feel unnatural (dystonic)

'Ego' with negative thoughts feeling unnatural (dystonic)

Negative thoughts no longer apart of the 'ego'

Sit comfortably in chairs facing each other, only about a foot and a half to two feet apart. Make soft eye contact with each other. See in the other a golden light that seems to come from their centre and radiate outward, very much as portrayed in medieval portraits of saints, with the exception that the golden light is not merely around them, but comes from someplace deep in their core and radiates outward.

Decide which of you is Partner A or Partner B. First, let Partner A see this golden light radiate from deep within himself. Partner B also visualizes the light coming out of Partner A. Continue this for about 30 to 45 seconds with your eyes wide open, although if it's easier you can do it with your eyes closed. Then shuttle and Partner B imagines the light coming from their core and radiating outward, and Partner A imagines the same thing about Partner B. Shuttle back and forth every 30-45 seconds, for about three to five minutes. I would be very surprised if you didn't notice that you felt differently about yourself, you felt differently about your partner, and there was a marked change in the atmosphere between the two of you. Remember that becoming aware that there is a divine part in all of us is a spiritual aspect of self esteem.

Would you like to try one more? This is a simple visualization.

The cerebellar hemispheres are two egg-sized and - shaped structures on either side of the brain stem. The brain stem is the upward extension of the spinal cord after it enters the skull. It moves upward and slightly forward for about 3-1/2 to 4 inches. Shortly after it enters the skull, on either side are the cerebellar hemispheres. If you rub your hand over the back base of your skull, on either side of the midline, you'll find two little bumps. Those actually are little concavities on the inside of the skull that house the back of the cerebellar hemispheres.

Imagine a beautiful pink light filling each cerebellar hemisphere, and see etched in each cerebellar hemisphere the words, "I was born to love myself. I was born to love myself." Once more evaluate the change in your feeling about yourself, in your self love, before and after the exercise.

B. Love of Others

A second facet of love is the ability to love others, the love of others. Opening of the heart to self and to others is the only task. Opening of the heart to others is an important part of life. There is no joy in life without an open heart. When your heart is closed, you feel and act irritable. It looks very much like a low grade depression, in which you can function, but there is no joy to you or to anybody else around you.

A simple series of exercises to open your heart, at least temporarily, to enjoy that feeling of a more open heart, is to very simply place the palm of your hand on the centre of your sternum or breast bone. Without lifting your hand from the surface, slowly rotate the palm of your hand in a clockwise fashion, as if the clock were looking outward from your chest. Rotate it slowly, as if you were gently stroking velvet and wanted to feel all of the sensation.

What do you experience? Do you feel warmth in your chest? Do you feel pleasure? Does it feel better to look at living things, at human beings around you?

When you have experienced some opening and warmth as a result of this simple rotation, imagine that under that same area of your breast bone is a rose bud, a tightly wound rose bud of any color or hue that you find particularly lovely. Let it push up through the tissue, through the bone, through the skin, painlessly, effortlessly, and as it emerges through the skin let it open slowly, rhythmically into this beautiful rose, and imagine you can smell the delicious aroma coming from the rose. Perhaps you might want to repeat this image several times.

Again, see how you feel. Evaluate how living objects, especially people, seem to you. Do they look different? Does the light that enters your visual field seem different? I hope you have had such an experience.

An open heart is risky, is dangerous. The danger is that you will be hurt, that there will be pain. But without an open heart and taking that risk, life is a living death; life is a living emptiness. You move through life as a functioning zombie, never really tasting and appreciating the fullness of life. When I worked in a hospital, I occasionally met patients whose hearts had been so damaged by pain, that they told me they would not be willing to ever risk loving again for fear that if they were hurt one more time, the pain would be so unbearable, they would kill themselves. But in a way, they were already the living dead.

When you are hurt, it is very important, it is very valid,

to close down and withdraw for a while, to let yourself heal with time. But then it is vital that you are open again if you are going to feel the full joy and dimension of your humanness.

The more you open your heart to others, the more you need wisdom – the clear vision of what others are like – the more you need self esteem – the clear vision of who you are, an appreciation and valuing of yourself.

When you have this wisdom and self esteem, you can avoid, and protect yourself against other people's predation. It is very common for women with low self esteem and open hearts to be unable to protect themselves, and to attract abuse and become severely, almost fatally hurt. Abused adults signal that they are vulnerable to abuse – by language, by being too 'nicey-nice,' by body language, having passive and flaccid body movements, and out of awareness, unconscious mind projections that say, "I will accept love at any price, even at the price of abuse." Of course, this doesn't excuse the abuser.

If you are one of these people whose loving nature unfortunately attracts abuse, there are things you can do with this awareness to start to protect yourself.

A very simple visualization is to imagine yourself surrounded by lions or tigers or any predator-protectors that appeal to you, that you can imagine. They are all around you. they are your friends and protectors. And they will only allow people close to you, they will only allow input coming through to you, that is non abusive, that is wholesome and encouraging. Remember, if you are the repeated victim of abuse, you are unconsciously sending out messages that, even though you are loving, you will accept abuse. And it is quite possible to switch this around with the help of your protectors, to "I am loving and I will no longer accept abuse."

Another, more powerful, exercise, which is sometimes immediately healing, is to find a partner who you know would never abuse you. You become the abusee, and they become the playacting abuser. If you can, tell them the kind of abuse that you have accepted in the past, and if they are creative and intuitive, they can improvise. The abuser, carefully establishing that this is a therapeutic exercise, sends out a steady stream of abuse to the abusee – "You don't deserve anything. You're guilty, etc." Pay a lot of attention to which ones strike home, and repeat them over and over.

As the abusee, feel the punishment you accept from the abuser. But don't succumb. Play around in your mind until the abuser tells you that you are doing something that makes him feel that his abuse is no longer welcome, that he can't put his venom into it, that it doesn't seem that he even wants to say it anymore. And with his direction, stay in that altered state. You may drift away for brief periods, and his abuse may increase in power, but then find your way back until you can find that mental state, that altered state of consciousness in your mind which is sending out unconsciously a message that "I am a loving person. I don't accept abuse."

You may have to repeat this very powerful exercise several times before you can maintain an atmosphere around you that says that you will not accept abuse. It will be very interesting for you to encounter any abuser in your life once you have achieved this altered state of consciousness, and see that the person who was once so powerful in their ability to hurt you is ineffective and impotent.

Remember, no one can tell you how to make this change in your mind and consciousness, but that you do at some level know how to do it. You must simply experiment in your mind and in your thoughts until the person playing the abuser senses the change in the information in the atmosphere coming from you.

Were you able to create an atmosphere that turned off the abuser? You can. I hope you were successful. You don't deserve the abuse.

C. Attracting Love

A third aspect of love is attracting love to you. There are many, many lovely, loving, lonely people, people for whom love stays away or comes in tarnished packages. They are sending messages in many ways, including language, body posture, voice tone, mannerisms and thought forms to keep others away – or attracting love to them in a distorted form.

I'd like you to try an exercise, very simple, but it can be very poignant. You'll need a partner again. Sit in two comfortable chairs with your knees about a foot of a foot and a half from each other. Taking turns, you say to the other, "Love me." And they reply, "I love you." And you respond, "Thank you." And then the situation is reversed. They ask for love by saying, "Love me," and you reply, "I love you," and they respond, "Thank you." You shuttle back and forth for about 3-5 minutes.

See how you react. Is it hard to ask for love? Is it hard to receive love? If you are comfortable in both asking and receiving love, you're very lucky. If it's difficult to ask for or receive love, you have to start to wonder why there is such distortion in the God-given right to know that you deserve love, and therefore in a sense to ask for it, and certainly in your right to receive love.

After you have done this exercise, which should be done with soft eye contact, notice the atmosphere around you, between you. Notice how things look to you in the place that you're doing the exercise. Is your state of consciousness different? Always observe. Remember that it is in awareness and observation that the beginning of all change and transformation are based.

The most important parts of our lives are not under our control. We cannot choose when we were born and which family we are born into. We cannot choose whom we fall in love with. And we cannot choose, unless we end our lives voluntarily, when we die and how we die. We fool ourselves if we think differently. Our lives through large measure are not under our control.

We can't help or choose whom we fall in love with or whom we attract until our awareness and consciousness change.

I first learned this in a very vivid way when I was a resident in psychiatry at the Menninger Foundation. I was called in consultation by the medical service to evaluate a woman in her late forties who was in severe mental and physical distress. There was no basic physical pathology, but she was worn out and distraught. She was asking to go home, but the doctors knew she was not ready yet. In those days, there was the luxury of permitting someone to stay in the hospital just because they needed the refuge.

This lady's story was a remarkable one. She had picked five husbands in a row who became alcoholic, who stole all her money, and left her. When I heard this amazing story I realized that no matter how smart I was, how sensitive, how sophisticated, how well trained, if I went out into the world and tried to pick five men to fall in love with who would become alcoholic, who would steal all their wife's money, who would then leave the wife, that I couldn't find them. I didn't have that perception and skill. Yet she could do it with no effort, intuitively. Her key only turned in the lock of potential alcoholic thieves and abandoners.

What a remarkable consistency of ability! The poor woman didn't enjoy any of this, and indeed, she looked like she was a victim of the Holocaust.

I can tell you another story, very similar in a way, even though it portrays what seems to be the opposite, of a brilliant, attractive, successful, wealthy (although she kept the wealth secret) professional woman who was in her early forties, and had never had a date. If you met her, you would find her to be charming, delightful to be around, physically quite attractive, lively and sexy. But she had never had a real date in her life. How could such a thing happen? I had her do an exercise that I am about to present to you to help elucidate what there was about her and men that caused this to happen. What she came up with was, "Men are yukko!" which was said with great feeling. All the men in her life, her father, her brother and her uncles, were not terribly pleasant to her, and had given her such a negative attitude toward men that to her all men were potentially 'yukko.' In addition to which, she had an older sister who was mentally defective, and an unconscious message had gone out from both her mother and her father that she was never to fulfill her life with a partner until her sister had been suitably taken care of. And so this brilliant, attractive, charming and successful woman of forty-one years had never had a date.

Here is the exercise: Imagine with your eyes open that standing about a foot to two feet in front of you is the ideal lover for you. When you can visualize this person vividly, or as vividly as you can, close your eyes and try to imagine them with your eyes closed. When you successfully do this, with your eyes closed, take a step or two forward to stand in the spot where you imagined your ideal lover. Then allow the energy, the beingness of this ideal lover to surround you and to penetrate every organ and cell in your body.

How did you react? Was it comfortable? Was it uncomfortable? What made it so? Use any awareness, any learning as a lever to change your consciousness, your programming, so that like the rich, desirable, attractive, charming successful professional woman, you can not allow your programming to contaminate the fulfillment of your life and the ending of loneliness.

A healing variant of this exercise would be to imagine yourself without fear of being loved, or imagine someone in life or in art who has no trouble attracting love, standing in front of you. Do this first with your eyes open, then with your eyes closed. When the image with your eyes closed is as vivid as you can create it, step into the image. Feel the energy, the existence, of that person around and through

23

you. How does it feel? How do you react? Stay as long as feels useful, then step out of the image, taking only the parts of the experience that feel positive to you.

If self esteem is the foundation of life, and opening your heart adds joy to your life, attracting love to you enriches and makes full-bodied this love.

D. Divine Live

The fourth facet of love is Divine love. The experience of Divine love is a special and precious exercise that cannot be described, but only experienced.

If it's possible, do this exercise with a partner. Have your partner place the palm of their hand in the centre of your spine, opposite the centre of your sternum or breastbone. Have them rotate their hand, slowly and sensuously, as if they were stroking velvet and wanted to feel every sensation, in a clockwise manner, without lifting their hand off your skin or clothes. It should feel very wonderful, and very peaceful. Rotate the palm of your hand over the centre of your sternum clockwise, the clock projecting forward from your chest, as in the opening of the heart exercise, *Page 17.*

Imagine that the full depth of your chest becomes hollow, almost as if there was a huge pipe that had taken the place of your chest and lungs, a big, empty pipe. As you breathe, imagine that on the in breath, the breath is moving from the back of the open pipe to the front. As you are breathing out, the breath returns from the front of the open space backward.

Once you are comfortable with this experience, imagine that from somewhere out in the Universe, a current of Divine love undulates back and forth with your breath. As you breathe in, it undulates from the back of the opening of your chest to the front. As you breathe out, it moves from the front of your chest back.

Once you are comfortable in achieving this imagining, then picture that with each breath in, this facilitates the flow of divine love from somewhere in the Universe to move continuously from the back to the front. And then even with the out breath it continues to move – that both the in breath and the out breath facilitate the flow of divine love from someplace beyond you to the back of your chest, flowing through your chest and out from the front of your chest into the Universe.

Continue this visualization for three to five minutes.

You can also do this exercise by yourself, leaving out the partner's contribution.

Not everybody will successfully achieve the goals of this exercise. Not everybody is at any one particular time ready to feel this flow of divine love through them. But the exercise can be periodically repeated until the experience is achieved.

If the exercise is successful, you will feel peace. Indeed, you will feel something that can only be called bliss. Any false sense of self will drop away. Look for signs of egotism, of self-centredness, or any false sense of self, and it will seem powerfully, yet comfortably diminished. There will be an absence of fear. Look for fear, and you will find that in this flow of divine love, fear is gone, egotism is gone, and bliss is the state of awareness of your being in this world. Look around you. See how other people, other living objects look to you. Does the light in the room look different? Does being in the room feel different? Remember how I started this chapter out – that love is a divine, cosmic energy which integrates with our individual vital life force and expresses itself as an emotion.

Love is a divine, cosmic energy which integrates with our individual vital life force and expresses itself as an emotion.

The many facets of love are potential barricades and barriers, and potential assets, on your journey along the Healing Road.

25

CHAPTER TWO

The Deterioration of a Loving Relationship, and Its Healing

A. Romantic Love and True Love

Relationship love is carried on the wings of true communication, with all the somatic and sensual feelings that accompany the experience of true communication. True communication exists when one is free to share their thoughts and feelings in an uninhibited, uncensored manner, with no motivation other than to share their thoughts and feelings with someone who is interested only in receiving and listening, uncritically and responding in a similar manner.

Wherever true communication exists, there is love. **Wherever true communication exists, there is love.**

All our experiences of love are basically the same. I believe we love people more, or less, but not really very differently. The kind of love only appears to be qualitatively different. The quantity of love is affected by the time we spend with the person we love, the intelligence, attitude and values of that person, and what we feel is appropriate with that person. Experiences and thoughts appropriate to a lover would be unfair to share with a child.

The following is an exercise in true communication. You will need a partner. Any partner will do. Now you have to decide who is A and who is B. Partner A makes a one-line statement. It can be any statement about anything. An

26

example would be, "The sky is blue." Partner B guesses the true meaning of the statement. For most statements there is a variety, a radiance of meanings around the statement called the metacommunications, or the penumbra of the communication. For example, with the statement, "The sky is blue," the metacommunication might be, "I miss seeing blue skies in Ireland," or "I think this exercise is very silly."

When Partner B makes a guess, Partner A can only reply with yes or no – no other statement, no other clues. The exercise continues until Partner A agrees that three yeses have been achieved. Then the roles are reversed and the exercise is repeated.

Did you have the experience of giving three yeses rapidly in a row? How did it make you feel? Did it make you feel lighter? Did it make you feel happier? Were there any feelings of warmth in your chest or your abdomen? Most likely, something like this happened to you. This experience of pleasure is an experience of love, the beginning of love, even if the exercise was done with someone you have never met before.

Were there a lot of nos? Were there many nos mixed with an occasional yes? How did you feel? I suspect you felt cut off, that there was a discontinuity between yourself and the other person, perhaps a feeling of frustration and irritation, as the possibility of love, the experience of love, was lost. In much the same manner, love dies between two people who previously knew and shared the pleasure of love.

Whenever there is love, there is a welling up of a feeling of well being, of warmth, usually in your chest and upper belly, a feeling of lightness, of joy, a desire to be physically close, or to touch, which can lead to a crescendo of sensual desire. The desire to touch is an aspect of communication and love just as natural as the grooming behavior is a part of the relationship of our simian, our monkey relatives. I believe the desire to touch, growing out of communication – or the illusion of contact and communication – is biologically based.

Children who are not touched often wither and die as their immune systems deteriorate. There is a very well known study by the famous French child psychologist, Piaget, of a nursery run by nuns in France that had an enormously high death rate among its orphan children. The nuns were meticulous in keeping the children clean. The nuns were perfect in providing the necessary nutrition to sustain the lives of their charges. And yet, the children died. What Piaget found was that the nuns never handled the children. Even feeding was done by a device that propped up the bottle so the baby could nurse.

Piaget recommended that the children be held when they were fed, and played with – and the death rate diminished. In Bellevue Hospital, in New York City, there was a very high infectious death rate in the children's ward that was almost completely reversed when lively and delightful young teenage girls were allowed to come in and play with and touch and hold and feed the children.

There was another famous experiment of the Rhesus monkeys and their cloth and wire 'mothers.' Baby monkeys were separated from their mothers shortly after birth, and divided into three groups. One group was fed and watered and nothing else was done. There was no companionship, no touching. these monkeys grew up to be neurotic, disordered monkeys. A second group had placed in their cages a wire sculpture shaped like a mother monkey. They were fed and watered, and grew up to be disordered, neurotic, dysfunctional monkeys.

A third group had placed in their cages a wire sculpture of a monkey mother, but this time the sculpture was covered with a soft cloth. The behavior of the baby monkeys was very interesting. They spent a lot of time cuddling in the soft cloth of the imitation monkey mother, and then would slowly explore the environment of their cage, and when they became afraid, would run back and cuddle in the soft cloth once again. Little by little they learned to feel comfortable exploring the furthest reaches of their environment, and grew up to be well adjusted, normal monkeys, able to take care of themselves and to relate comfortably with other monkeys.

These tactile and sensuous desires are part of every human love experience – between male and female, female and female, male and male, adult and child, human and animal.

All people falling in love experience the intense feeling of contact, or at least the illusion of contact, with the loved one. To some degree, the lover must feel that he or she has found someone who understands, whom they can be honest with, with whom they can make themselves vulnerable.

It's important to know that we can't help who we fall in love with. It is an unconscious process, conditioned by experiences around love and relationship from the moment we enter this world. Falling in love is very much like the relationship between a lock and a key. If the key has the right series of bumps and depressions that match those of the lock, the lock will turn; we will fall in love. This is pre-programmed – we will fall in love again and again, with the same 'lock,' with the same person, until the program has changed. The only freedom of choice we have is to decide, not who we fall in love with, but whether we wish to pursue the loving relationship. But is all love true love? Obviously not. There is instead the illusion of love, romantic love. The feeling of becoming one with the other. The feeling of having one's life instantly fulfilled with the other. The fantasy of fusion, of confluence, of oneness with the other. The fantasy of loss of self within the relationship. This substitutes for communication and knowing. It substitutes for true love.

I have often said that intimacy produces insanity. This breeding of insanity through intimacy is a result of romantic love. We are craziest with those we are close to because of the unreal illusions and expectations, often stemming from childhood, that are so much a part of romantic love.

Adding to the intensity of the insanity is that couples in

trouble not only have a false picture of each other, illusions about each other, but couples in trouble have similar basic problems, so they can't teach each other and can't understand each other.

This reminds me of the story of Peter and Phyllis, who came to see me, bitterly angry at each other, fighting almost all the time. They wanted relief from this living hell. Peter complained that Phyllis was physically cold to him, and almost always rejected his sexual overtures. Phyllis complained that Peter was never as loving as kind, or as patient as she needed. Phyllis knew, and was comfortable sharing, that she rarely felt any sexual desire and had little interest in that level of intimate contact. Peter presented himself as a frustrated stallion, a stud whose passion was constantly being negated and crushed.

As part of their treatment, Peter and Phyllis joined a couples group that I was running. With the experience of sharing their difficulties and the difficulties of others, and with the active encouragement of the other women in the group, Phyllis, who had a very traumatic childhood around sexuality, was encouraged to allow herself to feel for the first time the beginning of her own female passion and desire. It was a very precious thing, watching the women help to heal one of their sisters. Phyllis approached Peter lovingly and sensually in the group. It was a moment of human and therapeutic triumph.

Expecting Peter to welcome this new freedom and experience of hers, Phyllis was stunned at Peter's reaction. Verbally, and with the language of the body, Peter rejected her, pushed her away – totally outside of his consciousness, in speech, in tone, in behavior, he rejected her new freedom, which he had protested mightily was exactly what he wanted. It became very clear that Peter and Phyllis were more alike than had first seemed obvious, that Peter was as frightened of having a loving and intense sexual relationship with his wife as she was. And so a great deal more work needed to be done.

Romantic love, the love of illusion, is a seductive alternative to real love. Romantic love is intoxicating. It is said that in romantic love, chemicals are released into the blood similar to those released by eating chocolate, similar to endorphins. We all know how addictive chocolate is.

For a while, romantic love provides a feeling of warmth and a desire for physical contact, a feeling of total fulfillment. Most of our loves are a combination of true and romantic love. The percentages of each is what is important.

True love is a genuine knowing, romantic love an illusion of who the other is. For those of you who are fans of the television program Star Trek, romantic love is the holodeck of love. The more intimate a relationship, particularly one contaminated by romantic love, with its unreal expectations and fantasies, the less likely you are to be correct in knowing what the other person thinks, feels and believes. This is particularly true as the relationship gets into trouble. Never assume with someone you're close to, when there is a difficult situation, that you really understand what they're saying. Always check your beliefs and assumptions out. Always ask for confirmation that you are really understanding what your partner is saying.

The Deadlier of the Species was about to launch a murderous attack on her husband because of the 'nasty look on his face.' He protested his innocence, in the face of her loud, nearly physical assault: "A nail just came through the bottom of my shoe and stuck in my foot!" "*I* know hateful contempt when I see it," she replied. My firm therapeutic hand and the removal of his shoe definitively confirmed his statement.

Couples rarely look at each other when they are talking. In an intimate relationship, particularly when there is trouble, it is important that discussions, even arguments, do not take place from separate rooms, and that each participant looks at the other to maximize the possibilities of correct observation, and minimize the possibility of incorrect assumptions. When there is difficulty in an intimate relationship it is much more important that communication be very complete and detailed. If you get up in the middle of an argument to leave the room, it is important to say, "I'm not abandoning you; I am going to the bathroom. I'll be back." The more there is disharmony, the more it is necessary to rely on accurate information and to avoid assumptions, to ensure that there is a minimum of possibility that you are dealing with fantasy. Any discussion or argument based on fantasy can have no positive resolution. Remember, *any argument based on assumptions and fantasy, on illusion, can have no positive resolution.*

Most people have heard that in a therapeutic situation, the patient very often falls in love with the therapist. If this ever happens in my office, I usually respond in the following way: "That's wonderful. We all need all the love we can get. But please tell me what's wrong with me. Please tell me what my weaknesses and flaws are." If the patient tells me that they see no flaws, that I seem wonderful, my response is, "Ah, that is romantic love. You have an illusion of who I am." If the patient can clearly see my weaknesses, my peccadillos, my neuroses, then I know that something like real love has happened in the therapeutic communication.

It is no wonder that something that looks like love happens in the therapeutic situation. It is very unusual in this life to have anyone listen to you and respond to you uncritically for 45-50 minutes once a week. Can you guess how much time people who have been married for 10-15 years spend talking to each other during the week? One study in the United States came up with the figure, not of 2 hours, not of 1 hour, not of a half hour, but that couples spoke to each other only **14 minutes a week**. And much of that conversation was about the fact that the mortgage needed to be paid and the garbage needed to be taken out.

I'd like to tell you the story of a couple I had in treatment. She saw him as a brilliant, creative man. She believed that through him they would have a gay and intellectual life, traveling in brilliant and elevated circles, surrounded by shimmering events and people. He saw her as a woman molded to him, never contradicting him, looking adoringly at him – "You're right. You're wonderful. You're brilliant, darling."

But time, the great spoiler, intervened. She found she had married a brilliant but ineffectual man, retreating from life and challenges, finding it difficult to support his family. She became angry, bitter, bitchy. Thus did romantic love die a bitter death for both participants, he in shock at finding her to be very different that he had expected.

In romantic love there is no true communication. There is a denial of individuality, an attempt to confirm both partners' illusions. As romantic love decays, there is an increased feeling of emptiness, loneliness, frustration and anger. Depression and anger replace passion. This has to happen. This must happen. Because sometime, some place, reality intrudes. Illusion is harder and harder to maintain, eventually collapsing.

Part of the stripping of illusions is also that the person you fell in love with, in reality, is not the person you're living with in five years. People change and grow. After five years you are not married to the same person you first started out with. A wife seen as perfect and problem free, a wife who was raised to pretend that she was the perfect daughter and therefore the perfect wife, feels loved for a while until that love is eroded when, in her humanity, she needs and wants to share problems, and her surprised lover doesn't want to hear or know.

If, as occasionally occurs, a stable marriage is based on illusion, at least one of the partners severely sacrifices their individuality, and becomes an intellectual and emotional vegetable, a common occurrence in females who mold themselves to their husbands, and thus the sensuality in the relationship vanishes, and depression takes its place.

I know of a perfect marriage based on illusion, the father very much the head of the family, the provider, the decider.

The mother seeks only to please him, seeing that the children conform to his every wish. But she became a nothing, a no one, and he was no longer attracted to her, having instead outside affairs. In a similar couple, when their daughter married out of their religion, the father was angrily against it. The mother supported her daughter, but said nothing, kept quiet, and in her stifled, submissive anger, suffered a heart attack.

In a good marriage, as each illusion disintegrates, it can be replaced by an honest knowing of the other. In the relationship in which the husband saw the wife as perfect, when this illusion decayed, he could still appreciate all her positive traits and learn to become compassionate about her imperfections. So the marriage can grow and romantic illusion be replaced with true love.

What often happens instead, as illusions fade, is, "You're not the way you should be. You're not the way you gave yourself to me. You're not the way you were when we got together. I am betrayed." And what happens to a betrayer? In any social system, for a betrayer no punishment is severe enough. "I will force you to go back to my illusion of you, my image of you." And so a power struggle and rage and manipulation replace love. If this is not transcended with knowing, rage and murderous feelings ensue, and there is a constant, deadly anger. The relationship is over, destruction and chaos take its place.

The symptoms of a severely deteriorated romantic relationship are very common. There is a great deal of criticism, there is defensiveness, and even worse, contempt and withdrawal. There is nothing so final as withdrawal. There is nothing so deadly to a relationship as contempt.

If illusion is replaced by knowing, we have to decide if the new awareness and vision of the other is desirable and nourishing to us. If the answer is yes, communication becomes clear, love and sensuality flow. In a way, we must have many marriages with the same person, a kind of serial polygamy, serial marriage, with the same person – that's

34

naughty, and moral and exciting, all at the same time.

Because many of our expectations of love are based on childhood experiences, unfulfilled childhood experiences and childhood fantasies, adult love will never fit the picture that we bring to each other. So, out loud, say to your partner, "No matter how much I deserve it, no matter how much I want it, I will never be loved and cared for in exactly the way I imagined I would be loved and cared for." Say it again: **"No matter how much I deserve it, no matter how much I want it, I will never be loved and cared for in exactly the way I imagined I would be loved and cared for."** Once you accept this, you can move into accepting the joy of the love that *does* come to you. You can get part of what you had hoped for. But you may also get a great deal of love that comes in a different shape and a different package than you expected, and a lot of that may be a great deal better than anything you had anticipated.

If you have a partner, can you recognize any illusions that you had regarding your partner, that time and experience have illuminated with the truth? If you have the time and the inclination, write them down. Would you describe your partner differently now, than when you first got together? Write two descriptive paragraphs. You might entitle them Then, and Now. Young lovers, do you see the chaos of relationships around you? Yours will be different, right? Didn't the couples living in the relationship chaos have the same dreams as you at one time? Enjoy your love, young lovers, and go slow, and observe. You might write down everything that you love about your partner. Then list all their flaws. Share your list, your description, with your partner. See if they agree. Have them do the same with you. Can you role-play your lover describing you, and your major and minor characteristics? Do they agree with your portrayal? Have them do the same to you.

If there ever is a serious, persistent disagreement with your partner, present your partner's position to them as concisely and accurately as possible. Do they agree? They can then state their position again, and you can again repeat what you have understood. Do this again and again until your partner agrees that you are accurately portraying their position. Reverse roles. You cannot say you love someone unless you can walk in their shoes.

Do people whose opinions you usually trust see your partner as you do? Will you even listen to them without resentment?

An acquaintance of mine quoted her father as saying that "Love is a misunderstanding between two fools." Have you noticed that each generation of lovers believes that they have discovered love, sex and romance for the first time?

True love is so much work, when romance is so easy and energizing. Besides, you have the same right as each generation before you to make the same mistakes and to learn from experience.

In a chemistry course in college, the safety instructions were to weigh the material on glass instead of the usual paper because the material, if exposed to any water, burst into flames. I somehow managed to forget the instructions, and someone turned on a faucet with considerable force fifteen feet away. One drop of water arched through the air, and with unerring, fatalistic accuracy, dropped in the middle of my experiment, which burst into flames. "Some people have to learn the hard way," my patient professor remarked.

Pick a partner, preferably someone you love, but it could even be a stranger. Make eye contact, and sing together a chorus of "They say that falling in love is wonderful, wonderful, in every way, so they say." And now a second chorus – remember, the eye contact is important – "Falling in love with love is falling for make-believe. Falling in love with love is playing the fool."

Now, if you are lovers, take some time to go somewhere alone and enjoy each other.

Some acquaintances of mine had a very unusual way of handling their relationship. Before they decided to live together, without the benefit of formal marriage, they sat down and wrote a contract. In this contract they placed everything they thought would come up during their life together, and how they expected it to be handled – how finances would be handled, how disposing of the garbage would be handled, how making of the bed would be handled, how cleaning up of the bathroom would be handled. They discussed each point, wrote it out, signed the document, and started to live together.

At the end of each year they tore up this agreement and together decided if they wanted to recommit, to live together for another year. Until the last time I had contact with them, each year they decided to recommit to live together for an additional year. When this decision was made, they rewrote the contract, each and every year, adding and subtracting details and agreements based on their experience of the previous twelve months. The spirit of this attitude helped to keep their relationship alive. They recommitted every year with a clear understanding of how they were to live together, so that there were fewer areas of misunderstanding, unreal expectations and conflict.

This is rather an extreme way of handling the situation, and is not for most of us. But the principles involved apply to each and every one of us. It sounds unromantic, but indeed, it can provide a base from which true love, with a minimum of conflict, can evolve.

As illusion fades and reality intrudes, if we like what we see, we recommit ourselves to the relationship. This is the only way that sensuality and sexuality can be maintained over time. We have many loves with the same person. None of this is easy. Whoever said it would be? Maintaining and deepening a love relationship is the hardest task of life – the hardest and most important task of life. Romantic love is like the blazing up of a new, roaring fire. True love is like the warm, persisting radiance of the glowing embers.

B. Sustaining and Deepening a Loving Relationship

Your committed loving relationship is the most important part of your life for finding, for having, a happy life. The hardest task you will ever face in life is having a good marital relationship. It is harder than developing the theory of relativity or rocketing to the moon, or becoming a nuclear physicist. It is the most important part of life, but one we usually are least prepared for, unless you are one of those rarely fortunate individuals who came from a mature, happy and stable family. Movies and books don't help very much, and they often hurt. Have you noticed that the crucial things you have to learn in life are rarely taught? For example, whatever makes you a good doctor or a good psychiatrist is not taught. In school you learn a lot of things, but not the crucial learning for success, for being outstanding in your field. I am certain that the same is true for farmers, for shop keepers, for everyone. It is a strange rule of life.

What are the qualities needed to sustain and deepen a loving relationship? I call them the twelve commandments of intimate living and loving. If you can accomplish even 2/3 of this difficult list of necessary attitudes and traits for sustaining and deepening a loving relationship, you are a gifted and fortunate person who will have a very happy life.

1. Valuing Love

Love is the centre of life – the most important thing in life. This must be known. This must be appreciated. No life moves along its path with any certainty unless this knowledge is deeply felt and activated, used. There is much teaching that other aspects of life are of primary importance – acquisition of wealth, power, respect, health and long life. Many of these teaching have value, but none are central. None are at the core of life.

A life that values and nourishes love at its core is a rich life. When two people come together to share their lives, there are many aspects and dimensions to that sharing. Unless each participant believes, therefore practices the belief, that love comes before anything – before making a living, before being famous, before providing even the material necessities for the family – then that life, that love, that relationship, is an empty shell, a flowering tree that never buds.

The first commandment might very well be rewritten as, "Thou shalt value love above all else."

When I was teaching at Yale Medical School, one of my favorite teaching assignments was working with medical students. They were a highly independent, outspoken and challenging group who pulled no punches and would say whatever they thought. Yale was unique among medical schools in that students took no regular exams and didn't have to attend any classes. So, if they came to your class, that was their way of telling you that they felt the class was useful, that you were teaching them something. I was very good at making contact with difficult patients and very rapidly evaluating their state of being in the world. To both challenge me and to help patients who were indeed difficult to help, the students would bring to my seminars more and more difficult patients. It became a matter of ego, a matter of pride on my part, that I could always make contact, get to know and thoroughly and carefully evaluate each such patient.

One day they brought in a 'street Black,' a formally uneducated, but street-wise man who, as he walked through the door, radiated paranoia, suspiciousness and rage. He was not eager to trust anyone.

The minute I saw him and sensed his presence, I thought to myself, "Uh-oh. This time I'm going to bomb out. This time I'm going to fail." I tried everything I knew to make contact with him, but nothing I did worked – until, in an unguarded moment, he let slip a hint that the only person he had trusted, in the vicious and degraded life of the street, had betrayed him.

I jumped into that opening with both feet. I had sensed his pain. In acknowledging his disappointment, his heartbreak, his pain, everything changed. Suddenly, instead of a hostile 'street Black' talking to a middle-class psychiatrist, we were two people whose lives were touching together, who were sharing their common humanity. The conversation became intense, pertinent, and so engrossing that I completely forgot that I was in a class with medical students whom I was supposed to be teaching something.

When it finally dawned on me that I was supposed to pay some attention to the students, with a sweeping gesture I pointed to them and asked my patient to tell the assembled students "What is life without love?"

There was no hesitation. In a profound manner, in a resounding voice, he said, "Life without love is a crock of shit." Our teachers in life very often come at unexpected moments and with unexpected disguises. Another important such moment in my life occurred on an Aer Lingus flight from Shannon to New York. I was assigned a seat next to a very rumpled, poorly groomed gentleman. I remember feeling uncomfortable at having to sit next to someone who looked so disheveled.

During the flight, when the in-flight movie was to come on, I found that my speaker was not working. He noticed my distressed and immediately offered to exchange seats with me so that I could enjoy the movie, in which he had no interest. I thanked him for helping me. In a quiet voice of profound truth, he said, "That's what we're here for." I felt ashamed.

A 70 year old Italian immigrant woman, working in the fruit orchards of New England, was hospitalized for depression. She barely spoke, and would not leave her bed, even to go to eat or go to the bathroom. The family consisted of an unmarried daughter and a 90 year old husband, lean and strong as an animal, still climbing and pruning trees.

When the 70 year old woman was mobilized and sent home, I had her accompanied by a trained psychiatric aide,

40

who lived with and observed the family. There was no love in that home, she observed, only work, food and shelter. The poor woman of 70 had no further motivation to continue her work, and collapsed in depression. The only way she knew out of work was to be ill, in this loveless situation.

When there is love, it provides a foundation for any difficulty or disagreement to be corrected. In that love, there is happiness, peace, strength, wisdom and healing.

In my training at the Menninger Foundation, I was assigned to evaluate a five year old boy who was diagnosed by our team as having minimal brain damage. He was the most delightful, sweet and constructive personality any parent could desire. Many similar children, with equal amounts of minimal brain damage, who were evaluated, were unhappy, peculiar, almost psychotic, having been driven to perform by parents who were contaminated by expectations and ambition. The sweet child was the fortunate receiver of unconditional love, love that permitted his parents to sense his needs for extra rest, for slower physical maturation. Though this fortunate child was slightly behind his classmates in performance, he was ahead of them in sweetness, emotional maturity and sensitivity – not a tortured child, but a free child, a child healed and growing in an atmosphere of unconditional love.

How wonderful it would be if the great marketing and advertising networks of our county promoted love as the centre of life – not automobiles, or soaps, or lavish homes, or toothpaste, or cereals or nappies – but love as the centre of life. Perhaps the theme of their campaign might be "Opening of the Heart is the Only Task." It would include helping people to be aware of the sweet feelings in their bodies, and the warmth of relaxation in their chests and upper abdomen with love. They could demonstrate exercises that encourage the feeling of an open heart. But most of all, announcing clearly and concisely that you are a successful citizen of our society if you have an open heart.

The person who lives with an open heart, and values the

open heart as the most important thing of life, is immersed in the flow of divine love.

2. Union and Autonomy

When two people come together to share their lives, each such event, each such union, is an important event in the history of our race. Every culture celebrates this coming together, indicating how important such a coming together is in our lives, in the perpetuation of our race. The new unit is even considered holy because it is a perpetuation of life. A new unit is formed. It is a time of great hope, and so we celebrate.

If we think of each individual as a circle, when the circles come together, what form do they take? Do the circles overlap totally, so that there is one new circle where before there were two? Do the two circles overlap partially, and where they overlap a new structure is formed, with part of the original circles intact? Do the two circles press together and bend each other into a new shape? Or do the two circles touch gently at their edges and remain distinct? *[Diagram C – Romantic Love and True Love]*

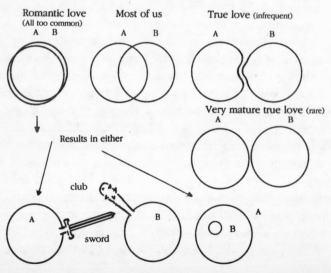

As infants we are born into the world with limited awareness of all the parameters and boundaries around us. A child feels oneness with his world, the world of himself, his mother, her nourishing breast. In that bond of necessity and love between mother and child, the new person is nourished and loved, experiences love, without any sense of separateness from the rest of itself that we call mother. As the infant becomes child, as the child becomes youth, as the youth becomes adult, a separation of boundaries moves to become established.

In most of us, the separation from mother and the experience of personal autonomy and love, have never been completely achieved. It must be a very difficult separation to make, since so rarely do we find autonomy, separate boundaries and the experience of love existing together. That is why it is said that for most of us, we usually marry our mothers.

For most of us, the separation, the autonomy, happens only in part. It is this heritage that we bring with us when we join our lives together with another person.

In 1972 I travelled to Japan and gave a lecture on the cause and treatment of disordered marriages to a group of Japanese therapists. After an initial reserve, there was a tremendous outpouring of interest and enthusiasm – questions, requests for exercises and experiences clarifying the nature of the marital relationship and its disharmony were endless – until, in exhaustion, I was forced to terminate the lecture.

I was then invited by several Japanese therapists to lunch. I asked them why there was so much interest in my presentation.

They told me that prior to World War II, marital disharmony was a negligible factor in Japanese family life. Since World War II, new phenomena had emerged that they did not understand. Prior to World War II, marriages were arranged by the parents. These were political and economic unions. Often the bride and groom did not meet before the ceremony, or at best met a week or two before the marriage. If the parents were loving and compassionate, they attempted to find a union which was not only politically and economically wise, but in which they felt the participants could find pleasure in each others' company.

The roles in marriage were clear. The husband's job was to support and protect the family. The wife's responsibilities were to maintain the home and to provide children. Love in no way entered the picture. Sometimes, over many years of sharing their lives, a gentle, true love emerged. But if this did not happen, it was of no importance. The husband found romance and excitement in affairs with public women, which were sanctioned by the community. In fact, it was a sign of wealth and status. The wife's only reliable source of love was her relationship with her children. Since love in no way entered the arena of marriage, the problems of loss of boundaries, of separateness, the historical remnant of the original mother and child bonding, did not enter this arena. There were almost no public marital problems.

After World War II, many young Japanese started to emulate the victorious Americans, falling in love, making choices of their own, and coming together with or without the blessing of their families. At the time of my lecture, the Japanese therapists told me that about 50% of marriages were of the new kind.

Within a short period of time, perhaps two years, what had seemed like a blissful decision became pure hell. The tortured couples were turning to Japanese therapists, psychologists, for help. "We were in heaven, in bliss. And now we are miserable, fighting, angry, violent with each other. What is wrong? Help us." The Japanese professionals, totally unprepared for this shift in cultural phenomena, had no idea what was going on or what to do. When I returned to my teaching position at Yale, I performed a library search. I knew the Japanese were very industrious, and if there was anything to read to inform them, they would have taken advantage of it. But at that time there was very little written about the decay and healing of loving relationships.

In the United States, depending on the area, 50%-75% of first marriages end in divorce. It is my personal estimate, based on professional experience and personal observation, that at most 5-10% of marriages are truly happy, another 5-10% are quite good, with everyone else living in various states of unhappiness and misery.

There is a strange phenomenon in mating: we choose someone who has desirable assets and characteristics that we do not have, and then we attempt to force them to be just like us.

With the loss of boundaries, and the attempt to convert two people into one, comes an inevitable event that we call a power struggle. The attempt to dominate, the attempt to make the other a copy of oneself. This oneness worked in childhood. In adulthood it produces a living, interpersonal hell.

The universal characteristics of a power struggle fight are a knot in the stomach, an argument in which each partner justifies themselves, attempts to persuade the other of the incorrectness of their position, resulting in absolutely no healing, no hearing, no movement – only deadlock, anger, pain and frustration.

When you feel that knot in your stomach, you must know that you're in a power struggle, for which there is no true loving or healing resolution. The only sensible behavior is to stop that discussion, that fight, and separate with the agreement to come back later and try to resolve whatever issues are on the table in a more positive way.

You probably have experienced, as I have, being at a dinner table with a couple who were in a power struggle fight. Do you remember how miserable it made you, how it spoiled the meal, how your digestion was upset, how your whole sense of being was in discomfort and disharmony? You were only an observer of this terribly destructive experience that we call a power struggle. Imagine what's going on in the minds and hearts and bodies of the participants.

Another characteristic of the symbolic power struggle fight is that each participant has to be correct. A wise man has said that marriage is the only relationship where, if you're right, you lose.

In an autonomous relationship, each person is intuitively aware of themselves, and feels totally responsible for his or her own behavior and reactions – without blaming the other. When there is coming together, it is comfortable and fluid, the sharing of a joint enterprise. Each person easily moves apart into separate activity. Separate feelings, separate attitudes, separate thoughts, are all permitted. There is as much a sense of standing alone in the world in such a union as if one were separate and living alone – with the exception that you know that you have a very special, loving friend.

A union without loss of boundaries is not without the stresses and difficulties of life. But they are dealt with and transcended without ugliness, attack, or power struggle fighting.

A rough litmus test that may help you determine your symbiosis-to-autonomy ratio can be attempted with a very simple exercise.

Look your partner in the eye and say, "You're not my [wife/husband]. You're [Name], and I choose to live with you within the contracts and agreements we have made."

Did that feel comfortable? Can you de-wife or de-husband your partner? In the role of wife or husband the malignant seeds of symbiosis frequently find fertile soil. With separateness and true partnership, there is no sense of 'wife-ness' or 'husband-ness', or surrender of self within a role. As one woman put it, "It doesn't feel like I'm married to Tom; it just feels like I'm living with my best friend."

A teacher of mine once reported that his father, who must have been a very wise man, said to him when they were fishing together, "In life you wear many hats. Right now, I'm wearing the father's hat; you're wearing the son's hat. Some day we'll exchange hats." Husband and wife are only hats, under which Fiona and Mary, Brian and Liam, move through their lives.

Sometimes, when boundaries are severely ruptured and one person blends in completely and submits to the other, the effect is a tragedy that most of us have seen.

Don is a powerful and effective businessman, with many talents, strong beliefs, and a desire to control any kingdom he is part of. This has worked well for him in his business life; he is a wealthy man. In his marriage, it has produced an apparently seamless, trouble-free relationship. But look more carefully. His wife has no thoughts of her own, limited interests, lacks vitality, has a tendency toward depression. She has lost herself in his power. She has surrendered. There is stability and superficial calm. But if you knew her when she was young, you might wonder if some disease had not atrophied, shrunken her brain and personality. He has affairs, tastefully handled during his business travels, because there is no excitement at home.

It is only when there is a union in which boundaries are maintained that a sense of newness, pleasure and excitement can be sustained.

Can you guess the only place where there is a healthy loss of boundaries? Of course. The only place where boundaries can be deliciously lost is during the moment of mutual orgasm, at the end of a delicious sexual experience that builds with pleasure, in which initially each participant is aware of the distinct separateness, in joy, of his/her partner. During the moment of orgiastic bliss, there is a cosmic union shared with the partner – a very special moment from which separateness and boundaries once again slowly emerge.

3. Expectations

For most of us this is the most difficult of the commands to understand and to practice.

Love has no expectations. Love has no demands. In a relationship of equals there is no place for expectations and demands – only wishes, hopes, dreams, preferences, desires – no expectations or demands.

This sounds very much like what is called unconditional love, and indeed it is. When most people hear this idea, this philosophical position, as necessary for sustaining and deepening a mature love relationship, their immediate reaction is one of disbelief. How can you have an intimate relationship in the real world without demands and expectations? In truth, you can *only* have a loving, intimate relationship in the real world when demands and expectations are nonexistent. The minute demands and expectations are entertained, the love relationship of equals is no longer equal. What one has instead is a hierarchical relationship, a relationship from a position of unequal power: "I *know* what you should be doing." From this position of 'knowing what you should be doing' is created the platform that launches criticism and contempt.

Demands and expectations are appropriate in a business relationship. But love is not a business relationship. In a love relationship, when demands are not met, there is disappointment and anger. When expectations are not met, there is disillusionment, judgementalness, even feelings of betrayal and contempt. Remember, for the betrayer in what is believed to be a loving relationship, no punishment is too severe, until the betrayer lives up to demands and expectations. So love is subverted in issues of power and submission, power struggles emerge, and love dies.

When one has no demands or expectations of the loving other, each task is a gift given willingly, lovingly, and therefore is deeply appreciated. The breadwinner supports the family in love, not because of obligations and demands, but because of having the willingness and the capability to work to provide necessities and pleasures for the loved ones. The partner whose primary responsibility is the home cooks and cleans, not because of obligations and expectations but because of having the ability and time to provide nourishment and care for those who are loved. Each gives freely and joyously.

Should either partner falter in the tasks they have undertaken, there is no resentment or anger – only understanding and compassion. If the breadwinner becomes financially encumbered, there is no brutality or anger – only love, compassion, respect and support. If the keeper of the home does not have dinner ready, there is only patience and understanding. The world's work between loving partners will get done without expectations and demands. **The world's work between loving partners will get done without expectations and demands.**

In more and more families in contemporary life, partners share the home as well as the breadwinning responsibility. it is even more important, more essential to do this without expectations and demands, so that the freely shared labors of each are appreciated, and the inner opportunities for negativity and friction are avoided as demands and expectations evaporate.

The world's work will get done between loving partners without expectations or demands, in an atmosphere of understanding, love, appreciation and acceptance.

Expectations are not only placed on the other, but also on oneself. A common, brutally destructive expectation, most common among men, is that "I have to make you happy. If you are not happy, then I have failed. I feel guilty, and I resent you for producing that guilty feeling in me. Instead of giving you compassion for your unhappiness, I will punish you for it. I expect myself to make you happy, therefore I expect you to be happy, and there will be hell to pay if you aren't."

Expectations toward the self are particularly destructive in modern life among women, who must be breadwinners, wives, lovers, parents and homemakers – an impossible task. In their expectations of themselves they produce additional stress, self torture, fear, discouragement, exhaustion and a sense of failure.

Slavery accomplishes the world's work in suffering and hatred. Hierarchy and power accomplish the world's work in stress, joylessness and submission. Love, which can have no demands or expectations, is both the engine and the fuel to accomplish the world's work without stress, submission or suffering. It accomplishes the world's work in peace and enthusiasm.

4. Patience

Patience is an aspect of wisdom, wisdom being defined as the clear understanding of the nature of things, a clear understanding of how people, systems, things operate. If you are tuned into the natural rhythm of anything outside of yourself, and in that attuning accept that there are rhythms other than your own, you have developed patience. It is important to be aware of the rhythm of all things, and in this awareness, patience and wisdom flow together.

Spring will come and the flowers will bloom when there is enough light and warmth. Not accepting and attuning yourself to these rhythms can only cause discomfort and disharmony. This is even truer in human relationships, most powerfully in intimate human relationships. To want others – the rest of nature, the universe – to move in rhythm with your own rhythm is an extreme of egoism, so that patience, true patience, is a step toward egolessness. And impatience is egotistical.

Do you get impatient when your partner is somewhat clumsy in putting a key in the door and opening the lock? When dinner is not quite ready on time? When your partner cannot learn to dance as well as yourself? There are countless opportunities for the exercise of patience or impatience in an intimate relationship. No two people's rhythms can be identical. One of the great virtues of living alone is that patience is less of an issue or a problem. Each attunement to the other's rhythm, each attunement, creates an opportunity for kindness and communion that will be sensed on a level that calls forth a feeling of being accepted and loved. Even though you are a better dancer, you are accepting the rhythm of your partner, and your partner's time frame, your partner's own rhythm. Acceptance creates harmony, warmth, and deepens love. Impatience violates boundaries. Patience enhances love.

5. Gifts of Love

Many times you have heard the statement that in a marriage, in an intimate relationship, you have to make compromises. I would protest that no compromises are ever necessary or desirable. Compromises breed a sense of submission and dominance, of inevitable resistance and resentment, of unhappiness.

What else could take the place of compromise? I would offer in its place the gifts of love. In any situation in which partners have different and divergent wishes, they can evaluate how important their own longing is in comparison with the intensity of the desire of their beloved. When you sense that your desire is not as strong as your partner's, you accede to the partner, and in this accession you are giving a gift of love. If there are two movies playing in your community and you want to see one, and your partner wants to see the other, and you know that your partner's desire is more fervent than your own, you agree to go to your partner's movie – not because you are weak, not because you are submissive, but because you sense this difference in desire, and you want to be together. So you offer yourself, in your going to the other movie, as a gift of love which is given freely – and, most importantly, with no resentment. The true sign of a gift of love is the absence of resentment. The alternative is dominance, submission and power struggles.

It is only when issues are crucial that gifts of love are not appropriate. On crucial issues, for the quality of your life and your values, when there is disagreement, there needs to be a strong discussion, even a creative argument. Only when everything is cleared, and lit by the intensity and passion of these vital issues, can the issues be closed. Vital issues happen occasionally. There are endless opportunities for gifts of love when you live closely with someone.

Since gifts of love are given freely and generously, they result in an upward moving spiral, in which, after having received gifts of love, every fibre of yourself enjoys the pleasure of returning similar gifts, so as the giving intensifies, the pleasure spirals upward. In power struggles, the spiral of discomfort, to the point of hell, is called a vicious spiral, a vicious circle. Strangely, no one has named the upward spiral, in which gifts of love multiply each other. I take this opportunity to name such a spiral a delicious spiral.

Greg and Judy were having a vicious fight about the position of toilet seats in their home – a not uncommon marital battle ground. As I'm sure you know, all men tend to use toilet seats in an 'up' position when they urinate; women use toilet seats in a 'down' position when they urinate. Judy deeply resented finding the toilet seat in an up position. Greg was not about to allow any woman to control him or order him around.

This sounds comical, but the intensity of the struggle was vicious. Have you ever seen small articles in the newspaper, something like, "He didn't like her meatloaf, so she shot him"? We all know, with carefully analytical thought, that meatloaf was not the issue, that there was a deeper issue. Meatloaf was the final precipitating event.

People in disordered marriages rarely fight about the real issues. The fight instead is about secondary, derivative issues, so the argument can have no hope of resolution.

The issue with Greg and Judy was not the toilet seat.

Judy was living in a desert, looking for signs that he cared about her, that he thought about her, that he loved her, that he considered her, that she was, somewhere, as important to him as his career. Greg had a domineering mother, and no woman was ever going to control him or dominate him. And so this very basic struggle was fought to the death – well, to the near death – over the position of the toilet seat. It was only when Greg was helped to see that Judy was not trying to control him when she wanted him to put the toilet seat down when he was finished, but merely wanted some sign that he thought of her and her needs and her comfort –that he understood the true nature of her request. He then started putting down the toilet seat when he was finished urinating, a gift of love, and they lived happily ever after.

6. Accepting Pain, Fear and Vulnerability

A friend once told me that he was deeply in love with a woman, and they were getting married. I replied, "You are doing the second stupidest thing any man could do." Naturally, he wanted to know what was the most stupid thing that a man could do. To this I replied, "not falling in love, deeply loving, and making a commitment to the woman."

Along with love, companionship, pleasure and sexuality, inevitably there is pain, fear and vulnerability at every level. There is no one who can hurt you as deeply as someone you love. Carl Whittaker, one of the founders of family therapy, once told me that the only person in the world whom he feared was his wife, whom he deeply loved.

With the gift of love and sexual pleasure comes an incredible level of sensitivity. We all know that a stranger can do something unpleasant, and it is fairly easy to brush it off. A similar statement or act by your loving partner feels devastating. The same statement or act unfortunately occurring in the midst of making love is intensified tenfold. In good lovemaking, all the defenses are down. Women intuitively seem to know this better than men. That is why they need to feel safe and loved before they can be sexual.

What are the fears that often seem to accompany an intimate, loving relationship, with its inevitable vulnerability? I'll mention a few. "If I love you too much, if I'm too vulnerable, I'll be left alone. I won't survive without you. I'll die," – or – "You'll damage me in some way," – or – "If I let myself love you fully, I'll lose myself in you and I won't exist anymore." Marriage sometimes creates the fear of annihilation via intimacy.

You must accept pain, you must accept fear, you must accept vulnerability. You must accept pain as the price of love. It's a package deal; there are no exceptions for anyone. Some people are so badly damaged in their attempts to fulfill their needs, to fill their lives with love, that they come to a place where they will not risk loving again – "I can't afford to. If I try once more and I'm hurt once more, the pain will be so unbearable that I will not want to live. I'll have to die. To stay alive, to avoid suicide, I have to give up hope of finding love." What a desperate dilemma for a human being.

There is a way for each of you to strengthen your heart's ability to tolerate emotional pain. I call this the heart roots exercise.

First, stand up and walk around the room, with awareness. Be aware of your feet contacting the ground. Sense where the centre of gravity is in your body – usually someplace in the middle of your abdomen. Sense your own feeling of solidness, of having your place in the world.

Now, sit comfortably. Suck, indeed nurse like a hungry child, on your thumb or the fleshy part of your hand just below the base of your thumb. Suck in an intense and vigorous manner, until you notice that there is a subtle warmth around the area of your heart.

When you experience this feeling of warmth, imagine that from this warmth, roots are nourished and start to grow from your heart. Let the roots go down from your heart through your chest, from your chest through your abdomen, from your abdomen to your pelvis, where the roots split up and move down each thigh, each leg, each ankle, each foot, until they are firmly anchored in the ground.

If you have difficulty visualizing the roots moving through any part of your body, such as the ankle, spend a little time rubbing, warming, relaxing that particular part.

Once the roots have entered the ground, imagine that they move more deeply into the ground, and then start to spread into branch roots and rootlets and root hairs, forming a deep ball of roots in the earth. Imagine the same phenomenon in your body, so that from the primary root that was nourished from your heart, rootlets spread out and divide, until every part of your body is grounded, both within your body and within the earth, through the roots nourished by the warmth around your heart.

Maintain the vigorous sucking and this image for about 3-5 minutes after the root structure is completed. If your lips become tired, rest them for a few seconds and resume sucking vigorously. Then allow yourself a moment and once again get up on your feet and walk around, in awareness.

Perhaps you feel closer to the ground, more firmly on the ground, contacting the ground in a new and better way. Perhaps you feel calmer and stronger. Do you notice that your estimate of your centre of gravity has moved closer to the ground, and in this movement you intuitively feel stronger and more solid?

Doing this exercise daily for 5-6 months not only increases your ability to tolerate emotional pain, but can change the muscular structure in your legs. For example, the patient that I first developed this visualization/meditation for had a 4th degree black belt in karate. Despite his expertise and skill, he had great trouble developing fully the muscles in his thigh. He had attempted this during years and years of intensive martial arts training. As he practiced this visualization/meditation for a number of months, he noticed that the muscular fullness that had eluded him for so many years had finally been created. In another patient, who spontaneously seemed to walk with her toes out, after a number of months of practicing this exercise – without any other effort on her part – she began to walk with her feet parallel and straight in relationship to her body and her direction of motion.

If you are fortunate and your relationship lasts and is a good one, as the degree of love and therefore vulnerability reach new and unfamiliar levels, fear and pain intensify – very often out of awareness sabotaging the deepening of love. You will try to stop this new level of vulnerability.

The fear and pain of loving is not a steady thing, but can go through periods of intense, sometimes volcanic-like eruption. One of the most consistent and fascinating phenomena in working with couples, trying to heal dissonance in their relationship, is that if the therapist is successful and there is increased tenderness, love and communion between the couple, at some point, disaster will strike. One or both of the partners, totally out of awareness, will do something incredibly devastating to the other. No warning stops this phenomenon from happening. Why should such a thing happen? Why should such a thing occur? It's really quite simple. When a marriage, a relationship, has deteriorated, both partners are deeply hurt and defended. (It is important that each partner know how deeply hurt the other is. Very often, they assume they are the one who is really hurt, and then attempt to inflict pain on the other to even the experience.) As the defenses start to melt, as the relationship heals, terror – unfortunately unconscious terror – strikes. Each person living intimately knows exactly where to provoke and injure the other. Do all of you know that? I'm sure you do.

Sally and Mike had a very rocky relationship. She was rather a strange, flighty lady, but not without her charms and delights. The stress of the marriage forced them to seek help. Intervention proved successful; there was less fighting, more tenderness, more lovemaking – when suddenly Sally did the one thing Mike could not tolerate. She went on a trip to New York City and had a one-night stand with a man of a different colour. There had been enough infidelity in the relationship so that if she had had an affair with someone of the same colour, this would have been uncomfortable but surmountable. Mike had no race or colour prejudice, but the one thing which she knew he could not tolerate was the thought of her suddenly giving birth to a baby of a different race. How could he explain that to the neighbours?

A couple whose relationship has severely deteriorated go through several such comings together and explosive separations before some kind of consistency takes hold. That's one of the reasons marriage therapy, even though skillfully done, sometimes does not heal the relationship. Many people are not willing to go through these explosions of pain, agony, even despair. This strange movement, this strange dance of healing and destructiveness, is intensified by the unfortunate fact that many couples only seek help when the relationship is almost over.

Although there are more sexual gymnastics in our society than there used to be, if you were fortunate enough to be someone who tries to help disharmonious relationships, you might think the opposite is going on. Many couples have not made love for weeks, months, years, sometimes for decades. They intuitively or consciously know that by decreasing the amount of pleasure between them, they are also decreasing the amount of pain and vulnerability. Early in my work with couples, when the work went well, I naturally would expect sexuality to rear its lovely head again. But often couples who had not made love for months or years would be tender, loving, cuddly, kind and considerate – but they would not have sex. No amount of instruction, analysis, urging, educating, understanding, would change this strange occurrence. The couple would support each other in making excuses, in finding reasons, why sex had not occurred. It might be many months, even years, before an attempt to be lovers is chanced once more. The partners, after having been in the hell that can only be created by the degradation of a loving relationship, are so happy to have kindness, tenderness, friendship and love in their life that they are not willing to take that extra step, that extra risk of vulnerability, that comes with sexuality.

Bob is an Episcopal priest, and his wife a musician. Their marriage had deteriorated considerably, and each had had outside relationships, but there was enough love that they wanted to heal the chasm that had developed between the two of them. Indeed that did happen. They glowed at each other. They cuddled in bed. They were tender and kind. But sex was not within the realm of possibility. They gave every excuse under the sun why the consummation of their reunion could not happen. They enjoyed the rekindled friendship, cuddling and verbal intimacy. Then Bob became a pastor at a church in a distant part of the country and they happily left the area together. Three years later I received a letter from him telling me that they had reconsummated their remarriage. I have no idea, besides time, what made this miracle take place.

It is one of the difficult quirks, one of the paradoxes of life, that pain must be accepted in order to have love. It is all right, in a state of pain, to withdraw like an animal into its lair and heal. But if you don't come back and enter again the state of vulnerability where pain can once more be inflicted, then you have committed yourself to a living death. There is no life without love, and there is no love without pain.

7. Compassion

Another wise man once said that you cannot say that you love someone and not listen to them compassionately. Listening is at the centre of love. Compassionate response to listening is at the centre of love. It is no accident of nature that women's hearing is more sensitive than men's. In their loving care of their children, mothers must be able to hear their children, all nuances of their children's crying, even when the mother is asleep. Compassionate hearing can be defined as hearing the other with total attention and a nonjudgemental attitude. The response to what has been heard shows that the content and overtones have been sympathetically registered.

When I first met Virginia Satir, a founder of family therapy, she was introducing herself to a group of participants in a workshop. She greeted each participant individually. When she spoke to me, a woman I had never met before, I immediately felt loved. I was puzzled. How could she love me? I've never met her before. She then went on to greet the next person. I watched very carefully; she seemed to love that person too. I finally observed and understood that when Virginia spoke to someone, she was totally present, totally tuned in, and totally listening and responding, in a caring, nonjudgemental way. She could do this better than any human being I have ever met. This is what I was confusing with love.

Indeed, it is not confusion. It is near the centre, the core of love. There are many facets of love, but such compassionate listening is essential to the experience and deepening of love.

Men, listen. All the great lovers of history were compassionate listeners. They were not macho heroes. To know the essence of love, to deepen and share the depths of love, the experience of mutual, compassionate listening is essential. The more you open your ears, your personality and heart to compassionate listening, the closer you move to being a vessel of divine love. In intimate living, compassionate listening in speech, conversation, brings a spark of divine love to human love. Someone has once said that the way to a woman's heart is through her ears, and that the way to a man's heart is through his stomach.

8. Kindness

A psychic and healer once said to me, "Harvey, you do not have to worry about going to hell after you die. This earth is hell."

Have any of you read the book *Wild Swans*, by Jung Chang? She writes about her experiences during the amazing Cultural Revolution in China. During the Cultural Revolution, half the world's population went mad. They tortured each other physically and verbally. People were killed, starved to death, humiliated. The economy, the health care of the country, deteriorated. All this was orchestrated by one man – Chairman Mao – in his desire to perpetuate his power. It is not only amazing that half the world's population temporarily deteriorated in this way, but that Chairman Mao was so knowledgeable and in control of his culture that he was able to bring this about without a secret police force. Even in the midst of this torture and chaos, Jung Chang noticed that there were two kinds of people. One kind were the people who either enjoyed or went along with the torturous instructions of Chairman Mao. But there was another kind of people, unfortunately rarer, who tried to find a way around the insulting, the humiliating, the physical and mental torture. She came to the conclusion that there are only two kinds of people – kind people and unkind people. I think she may be right.

What else can you say about kindness? Everyone knows when they receive it. Everybody wants and needs kindness. Kindness is a soothing balm for those aspects of hell that are part of our life. So much of the world is alien, indifferent, hostile and dangerous. Without kindness this produces a hell for us to live in. Kindness is the recognition that we are all fragile creatures. We are all fragile physically. Our lives can be snuffed out in an instant. But we are also fragile emotionally. We are easily hurt, easily damaged. Kindness is the recognition that this is true. And with that recognition, in a state of love, kindness automatically flows from us.

There is no relationship that is more fragile or vulnerable than that of two people who love each other. Love exposes the core of each of us, where we are like a delicate, fragile piece of coral, easily crushed. The true lover knows this and can only respond to it with kindness.

We were meant to live in groups – in families, tribes, in clans, where we were known to each other and every member of the group, tribe and clan. In such an arrangement, there was more of a feeling of safety, of being known, and at least the possibility of being treated kindly, an insulation from the possible dangers of the rest of the world. With industrialization, the tribe, the clan, and now even the family have largely become antiquarian relics, outmoded. And with that, a great deal of the security, safety and kindness have disappeared from the world. One of the pleasures of driving on the tortured roads in scenic rural Ireland is that on meeting, and successfully passing another vehicle, each driver raises his hand in greeting. It is an acknowledgement that we as human beings have politely, cooperatively and successfully shared a difficult situation. I hope this custom never disappears.

I ask each of you to make a conscious effort to make up for that lack. Bring kindness into your life and share it with others. Even in the simplest task or event in your life, such as thanking a toll collector. (What a boring, thankless job!) Kindness adds a little more security and positivity to the world. Let us move toward a society, toward a world, of kindness.

9. Tone of Voice – The Music of Love

In a loving relationship, the music is more important than the words. When the music and words support each other, the message is powerful, penetrating and clearly heard. In an intimate relationship, when there is dissonance between the manner of speech, the carrier, the voice tone and the content, it is the tone of voice that will be responded to, not the content. No matter how positive or noble the content, it will be impotent unless the tone, the music, that accompanies it, is also positive. Loving communication is more music than words.

Let me tell you the story of a piece of cherry pie:

A PIECE OF CHERRY PIE

"It certainly is nice to have Martha take dinner with us, isn't it, John?"

"It certainly is nice," he droned in reply.

"I find it relaxing to have someone else here. Not that I mind the strain. It's not that. I can take it. I have always been the strong one. I never know when something is going to happen, though. There's no sense to it. That's what makes it hard. John can seem as normal as he does now, then he suddenly changes. For no reason. You're feeling all right now, John, aren't you?"

"Yes, dear," he replied in careful cadence.

"You're sure, John?"

"I'm sure," he echoed.

"I just want to know for your own good. You're certain you're not feeling funny."

Again his agreement echoed.

"John, I wouldn't want you to say so just to make me feel better."

"I feel fine, dear," came the reply, carrying an exaggerated note of resignation.

"Well, if you're certain about it – " and she turned from her husband. "Martha, I always take good care of my husband. If there's one thing I am, it's a good nurse. I guess what happened has to do with the operation. John seemed normal in the hospital, though, after the hernia was operated. It first happened on his fourth day home."

She turned to her husband. He was sitting placidly at the dinner table, but with a hint of stiffness – like an Egyptian statue. "Would you like some dessert, dear?"

"No, thank you."

"I have cherry pie."

"No, thank you," came the even reply.

"You know you like my cherry pie, John."

"I'll have a piece, dear." His answers seemed careful.

"Besides, she added, "It's good for you. You need to build up your strength. Martha, being a real nurse, you know how uncomfortable a man can be after an operation. They're not strong like us women. We were sitting around after dinner, and of course, I was trying to make John comfortable. Wasn't I, dear?"

"That's right," the echo replied.

"Then he started to look funny. Kind of glassy, you know. Like he wasn't in the room. John – would you like a large or a small piece of pie?"

"A small piece, dear," he answered.

"How about a large piece. Cherry pie *is* your favorite."

The knife in her hand was held poised over the pie. She turned her attention to Martha, and didn't seem to hear her husband, when he answered, "A small piece will do."

"You wouldn't believe it, Martha, but he started to speak in a loud voice. John *never* speaks in a loud voice. Not in all our thirty married years has he ever raised his voice around me. He said the strangest things. The world is coming to an end! The bomb is going to be dropped! Everyone will be killed! We are all going to die! He seemed to be looking at me. Well, sort of – maybe kind of through me. I was frightened. Well, not really. John wouldn't hurt me. I would never be afraid of that. John – you do want a big piece of pie."

"That's ok, dear," he answered.

She lifted the knife on the pie, and spoke to her guest. "If there's one thing I know, it's that John wouldn't want to hurt me. What reason would he have? We've always been close. We never go anywhere alone. Always together. That's how close we are. I know John would tell you what a good marriage it's been. We raised two fine boys, both married and doing well. Is this piece big enough, John?" She measured off a restaurant sized piece.

"That's fine, dear."

"Of course, I was worried. I called the doctor. He came right over and gave John some pills. Are you sure you don't want a smaller piece?"

There was no reply.

"I want you to have the piece you want. Don't take a big piece just for me. Here I'll cut you a small one. You're sure that's all you want, though. You can have a bigger piece if you'd really like it. How about this big," measuring an imaginary piece with her fingers.

John slowly rose from his chair. He moved slowly, stiffly – mechanically – as if the motors of a hidden, mysterious force were lifting him. His face was wooden, his eyes glassy.

THE END

An intimate relationship is very much like a dance. In that dance, the partners respond to the rhythm and the music much more than to any content. The responses to dissonance in the music are usually instantaneous and destructive – rage, withdrawal, counterattack, sullen silence. It is necessary to have an instantaneous healing response when dissonance and disharmony are present. A very simple and effective technique is to have your partner agree with you on a neutral code word, preferably a single code word that will communicate to the other instantaneously and without distortion that the manner in which the message is being communicated is so disturbing that *it* is in danger of being responded to rather than the *content* being responded to. A very simple word would be 'tone,' but any word that can be said quickly, that is difficult to say in a nasty or an angry way, and that is agreed upon by the partners would be equally effective. 'Daffodil,' 'Daisy,' 'Mickey Mouse,' 'Minnie Mouse,' any word that is agreed upon will do.

Like music, the vibration of tone is listened to by the entire body, not just our ears. Our bodies are the product of millions of years of evolution, and have the wisdom of those millions of years of evolution – the wisdom to know when kindness and love are the companions of the message, or when anger and destructiveness are the companions of the message. The content is primarily decoded by the intellect, which is merely the product of a single lifetime. The message of the music, the tone, filtered through ages of evolution, is always clear.

10. Unfinished Business

Janet and Bob's marriage, or any hope for happiness in their relationship ended on their wedding night. They made love for the first time on their wedding night. The loving sexual experience was immensely powerful and pleasing to both of them. She was a virgin, and the magic and mystery and romance were overwhelming. She felt in awe of the experience. But Bob, relaxed by his orgasm, fell asleep. Janet was deeply hurt and resentful that he withdrew in sleep and was not awake to celebrate the majesty of the experience and the incredible gift she had just given him. She was angry and resentful twenty-two years later, when I first saw them.

Each wound, each hurt, in a loving relationship is multiplied many times by the vulnerability that comes with love. Each hurt that is not healed, expressed, transmuted, ended, is turned into a building block. Each hurt adds one building block to a wall that becomes a barrier between the former lovers.

Almost everyone, when they first get together, are filled with love and tenderness and sensuality, and great hope for the future. But as the wall of unresolved pain is built, the love and the sensuality slowly die. The great dissolution of sexual passion among couples in their forties is not the result of any hormonal phenomenon, but is largely due to the alienation of unresolved pain. Many happy relationships are thus ended on the wedding night, on the honeymoon.

But these are exceptions. Usually the building of the wall is a gradual task that is so gradually and skillfully and unknowingly built that the alienated lovers are even alienated from the knowledge of the cause of their unhappiness.

At first, the wall of building blocks made of unresolved pain reaches as high as our knees, and the formerly loving couple are less graceful in their movement together. Then it reaches to the waist, and sex dies. Then the wall is raised to the level of our chest, and love dies. As it grows higher and higher, the formerly loving couple cannot even see each other, and all that is left is apathy and estrangement.

The persistence of love and passion requires a constant weeding and cleansing of each fragment of emotional pain.

11. Establishing Communion

Communion can be defined as communication beyond the level of problem solving and shared interests – beyond the level of, "Is the mortgage being paid on time," or "Did you reserve a round for both of us at the golf course."

If no one can say they love unless they listen, when what is received and listened to is at the level of communion, the love is enriched and infinitely deepened. Communion is a sharing of the basic elements of our humanity. Communion is the sharing of our hopes, our pains, our fears, our humiliations, our foibles, our triumphs, our beliefs, our values. Communion is wondering together, from the centre of our vulnerable, frightened humanness, about the meaning of life and the meaning of death.

A psychiatric friend of mine once told me that he and his wife, every night when they go to bed together, share with each other the fears and humiliations of the day. Thus, they can get together cleared of this debris, but more important, having shared their human frailty and having had it received in a compassionate manner.

At a level of communion, a strange thing happens. Not only is love felt and enhanced, but time seems to disappear. Sometimes a few minutes will seem like hours, sometimes hours will seem like a few minutes. The very act of communion transcends the experience of time, and in that transcendence of time leaves us floating in the holiness of our shared humanity and love.

12. Trust

It is absolutely essential that you know – and that it be true – that next to yourself, your partner is the most important thing in the world, *and will treat you honestly and will live up to most of your agreements*. It is absolutely essential that you know and believe that your partner equally places themself first, and you, next to themself, before anything else in life in the world.

This is the essence of the level of trust that is needed. When there is lying, misguided dealing with money, infidelity, these are but secondary phenomena – secondary manifestations that the level of trust does not exist. Somewhere in the maze of the other eleven commandments the roots of the broken trust are to be found.

"I place you, next to my basic self interest, as the most important thing in the world, and I would like that from you." In that trust, the home becomes a castle, a place of peace, security and tranquillity in a disordered world.

Once the fabric of trust is broken, the healing is painstakingly slow. Love without trust is a disordered illusion. Love with trust is an oasis of peace and paradise in a world of uncertainty, a world of mottled trustworthiness.

The task of intimate loving is endless and complex and extremely difficult. The garden of love must be constantly weeded. But there is no other task as important or as potentially rewarding. Undertake it with resilience, courage and enthusiasm.

Chapter Three

Fear and Anxiety

How many of you reading this page suffer from more fear and anxiety than you would like to live with? I can picture all the hands being raised. Fear and anxiety are hell to get rid of. Would you like to lose all your fear and anxiety after reading these pages? I can imagine your cheers of affirmation. Well, that won't happen, but perhaps I can help you move along in that direction.

Imagine that you are walking down the street, and in your mind's eye that you are looking at all the people that you pass and in your mind imagine saying to them, "I'm afraid and I know you're afraid." You might want to actually try this the next time you're in town. If there are people in your life that you can do this with, making eye contact with them and saying, "I'm afraid and I know you're afraid," people who won't think you're too crazy, that also would be a useful exercise to perform.

Indeed, everyone is afraid. some of us know it and some of us don't. There is nothing to be afraid of. And that's the good news. The bad news is that it's very difficult to realize that there's nothing to be afraid of. I once told a friend there is nothing to be afraid of, and he replied, "that's the scariest thing I've ever heard." What could he have meant? I think he meant that we all have the illusion that fear protects us. The illusion that fear protects us is one of the most dangerous and damaging illusions in human life. Without fear we would change and move rapidly on our life's journey – and for most people that prospect is terrifying. Remember, there is no growth or change without fear. With growth and change we move into the unknown, and we violate often unconscious inner prohibitions that tell us to stay where we are, that to progress in our lives would be damaging if not lethal.

Find a partner. Sit comfortably opposite each other. Using your partner's name, say to them – let's imagine that their name is John – "John, there is nothing to be afraid of." His instructions are to reply, "Thank you," and then to repeat the same statement using your name back to you. Your reply again is "Thank you." Shuttle back and forth in this manner for about 5 minutes. How do you feel at the end of this exercise? Are you in an altered state of consciousness? Has there been any change, no matter how small, in the amount of fear that you live with? Evaluate the value of repeating this exercise on a regular basis.

This same exercise can be performed without a partner. Find a mirror – any mirror. Make eye contact with yourself in the mirror, and say to the person in the mirror, "There is nothing to be afraid of." You can do this with every mirror you come across, out loud where that's appropriate, silently in your mind where that is appropriate. A very useful and very intense way of pursuing the same healing of fear can be achieved by buying 4 cheap cosmetic mirrors. Most of the ones available have both a round and a square mirror. Buy at least 4, more would be useful, and place them strategically around the table with the square mirrors to the outside of the table and the round mirrors to the inside. Move around the table, and at each square mirror, make eye contact, and say to the person in the mirror, "There is nothing to be afraid of." Once you have completed a circuit of the table, then repeat the exercise with the round mirrors. If you can afford more than more mirrors, please do so. I would be very surprised if at the end of even a single experience of this exercise you did not feel different in a way that you would value as desirable.

I define levels of fear in kinetic-motoric form. Anxiety is a level of fear that we can move toward, even though it feels bad. Fear is a level of fear that we want to flee from, run away from. Panic is fear of such a level that we cannot move – we are in a state of terror – we are frozen. Horror is something else altogether. Horror is not an inner level of fear. Horror is our response to something that actually exists, that is not just of our minds. It exists externally and we have witnessed it – that is horror.

What are we afraid of? We are afraid of annihilation. Annihilation doesn't simply mean that we are going to be killed. Humiliation is a form of annihilation. Shame is a form of annihilation. Embarrassment is a form of annihilation. They all destroy us. They are all little deaths. They all compress us to nothing. We are also afraid of loss of what we have. We are also afraid of injury. From this point on I will talk of all these aspects of fear under the heading of annihilation.

Annihilation fear is behind what we call character and character formation, and behind all neurosis. Character is the collection of adaptive mechanisms that we have learned in our life experience that are designed to prevent annihilation, loss and injury, and to produce, hopefully, the most of life's goodies. They are the encrustation of years of learning and experience. If there were no annihilation fear, we would have no 'character.' That sounds strange, but it really is quite wonderful.

In my life I have met only one human being who had no 'character,' who simply *was*. I was lucky to meet him. His name was the Lama Govinda, the most remarkable human being I have ever met. Knowing him has created my model of a healthy human being, a human being free from 'character,' free from neurosis.

I met him quite by accident, at a professional meeting I was attending. I was so taken by meeting such a startling, unique human being that I avoided all my other activities and responsibilities at this meeting, to spend as much time as I could with him. **He simply was whatever he said.** He simply was whatever he said. He spoke clearly, concisely and with vitality – but with no desire to influence, alter, manipulate or impress. He simply was whatever he said.

The Lama Govinda, in his seventies at that time, was a wise, delightful old man, whose eyes sparkled and whose voice frequently laughed. He had a sense of humor and no ego in the sense of egotism. In the cleverest, sneakiest, most manipulative way that every ounce of my intelligence could muster, I attempted to trap the Lama into some expression of egotism. It didn't happen. It took no conscious effort on his part to avoid my tests. Surprisingly, even though he was in his seventies, there were no wrinkles in his skin. His skin had a soft, baby pink quality. It is my understanding that the few people who reach his level of spiritual evolvement and emotional cleanliness all have bright, sparkling eyes and soft, wrinkle-free, baby-like skin. Apparently their connective tissue does not age the way most of our connective tissues age.

The Lama Govinda was a Buddhist lama. He started life in Germany, where he wrote a Ph.D. thesis on comparative religion, and came to the conclusion that Buddhism was the only religion that made sense. Buddhism is unique among religions in that there is no god. Buddha says, "What I have achieved, you can achieve; you can be like me." It is the opportunity of all believers in Buddhism to follow the path of Buddha, to move and become themselves the Buddha.

When he finished his Ph.D. thesis, he became a Buddhist monk, traveling all over the world trying to understand the essence of Buddhism. He finally became a lama, or bishop, and had many adventurous travels in Tibet before the Chinese took it over. He was able to get into Tibet because he was a Buddhist. Just before I met him, an acquaintance of mine had found him sitting quietly in a shack on a mountain top in India, where local people would bring him food, as they do for all wise and holy men. He wanted to come back to the Western world to write and to publish, and so I had the opportunity to meet him.

The Lama Govinda had spent his entire life cleansing himself of fear, of mistaken thinking, mistaken values, and so was one of the few people that every hundred years reach that level of evolvement and health. Most of us, caught up in the struggle of making a living, raising a family, paying our taxes, can never reach his level. But he was very valuable to me, and I think to everyone, as a model of what a human being can be like, setting a direction that we can move toward, even though we never get quite as far down that road as he did. Travelers have always needed a stable star to navigate by.

Neurosis is the accumulation of learnings that are no longer adaptive, and are indeed destructive instead of protective or enhancing. Behind all neurosis is annihilation fear. These often unrecognized fears are believed, lived, and are maladaptive.

One of the reasons getting rid of neurosis, one of the reasons changing our character structure is so slow and difficult, is that we have to enter the valley of the shadow of the illusion of our annihilation – a terrifying journey requiring courage and commitment.

But there is nothing to be afraid of! All fear is unreal. **All fear is unreal.** Unreal fear destroys us. It destroys our freedom. It creates in us a false sense of security – the illusion that you are protecting yourself. It destroys our personality, keeping us from growing. Cultures stagnate and deteriorate because in the fear of change, they can't adapt. Wars are caused by fear. Without fear, wars would be unnecessary.

There is a strange phenomenon, based on historical precedent, that decrees that when physicians are being trained to be psychiatrists, they are placed on the ward with the craziest, most violent, most difficult to treat patients. That would be roughly akin to trying to train a paratrooper by throwing him out of an airplane without a parachute.

When you're placed on these wards, you are untrained, and feel very threatened and unprotected. Historically, this was the only place psychiatrists could have been trained. And even though the situation has changed, this is how their training begins.

When I was a first year resident in psychiatry at the Menninger Foundation, I had three goals. One was to learn as much as I could. The second was to make sure I really wanted to be a psychiatrist. And the third was not to get hit. Let me tell you a story that taught me how not to get hit.

On my ward was a short, wiry man, smaller than I was, but he had been a professional boxer. That made me wary of him. Indeed, one day he got me in a corner and started threatening me. I tried to calm him, using my best logic and dulcet voice tones, with very little effect. Finally I managed to escape and commandeered a number of psychiatric aides, who grabbed him and placed him into a treatment, which has largely become outmoded, called 'cold packs.' These are sheets that have been dipped in ice water. The patient, nude, is wrapped like a mummy in the sheets, and is first chilled to his bones, and then his body heat warms him up. The effect is very sedating, very calming, and you don't have to worry about the side effects of sedating drugs.

When I knew he would be calm, I went down to see him. What I said was, "Do you know what I'm going to do if you ever corner me and threaten me like that again?" He said, "What?" I said, "Well, you scared the hell out of me. I'm a doctor, not a boxer. Next time, I'm just going to run like hell." After that, we were comfortable with each other, almost friends. And maybe something therapeutic happened to both of us.

I learned that a patient only threatens you, will only injure you, if they are frightened of you. If you can reassure them that you are just as afraid, or in any way let them know that you are no threat to them, their violence disappears.

Politicians, bullies, control us, manipulate our lives –

even manipulate us to the point where we give away our goods and are willing to risk our lives in combat – because of fear. Fear makes us incredibly vulnerable to manipulation by others. If we could find a pill that had no side effects and would remove fear and anxiety, I believe that all of us would grow and change and become like gods, and that the earth could truly be transformed into a paradise.

What is the most paralysing fear? The most paralysing form of fear, I believe, is the fear of your fear. It prevents you from confronting your fear, from learning in any way that it is not real. You cannot deal with your fear. People who are frightened of their fear are trapped in life.

What drug masks fear most rapidly? Alcohol. Alcohol is not just a sacrosanct, almost holy social beverage. Alcohol is a liquid drug that can mask our fear quicker than any medical drug. One of the great dangers of alcoholism and heavy drinking is that you can never transform, confront or transcend your fears, so that no growth or maturity is possible.

The awful problem with fear is that it feels so bad. No wonder people handle it ineffectively.

What is the most exotic form of fear? The most exotic form of fear is the fear of *no* fear. That does happen. It happened to me once after a wonderful mystical experience, where for the first time in my life I felt no fear. And then after a period of several hours, I killed that experience. I brought that fear back. Why would I do such a stupid thing? I've wondered myself. In thinking about it, it became pretty clear to me that the illusion that fear protects was still a part of me. Most difficult was the awareness that there were no longer any limits in my life, that I could become almost anything that I wanted to be, that the parts of me that I had so treasured, as protecting me, as bringing me the good things of life, were no longer necessary. I was not ready to give them up.

The story of that experience might be of some interest to you. I had spent a weekend in chanting and meditation, felt it was useful, but had decided that not a great deal had happened. The next day, I was seeing my patients as usual, and at 11 o'clock – the memory is so vivid that even 15 years later I can remember the time – a patient of mine, a clinical psychologist of whom I was very fond, came to see me and was in a great deal of emotional pain. The nature of the pain was such that there was not much I could do but listen and be sympathetic. I was impotent to relieve his suffering. In the embrace of my impotence, a most remarkable thing happened. I suddenly felt that my chest had disappeared, and from somewhere beyond me, flowing through me was this intense current of love. The feeling in my mind and body was a state of the most remarkable well being that I can only call the sweetness of bliss.

I noticed soon after the experience began that I couldn't find my fear, the fear that had been with me all my life. I finally found a little bit, and the fantasy crossed my mind that the fear that was left was like a very tiny mouse and I was like a huge cheese, and that mouse could eat for the rest of his life and would never come even close to devouring that cheese.

Most remarkable of all, my patient immediately felt relieved of his pain and developed a clarity of thinking that permitted him to look at the situation that had caused the pain with a new, mature vision. I didn't have to do a thing. He was transformed in my presence. "Oh, my God!" I was an avatar, a person in whose presence people are transformed. I was an avatar for three hours!

The next patient I saw was remarkably improved without my having to do anything. All my training, knowledge and skill were totally unnecessary. I found it incredibly relaxing. How wonderful that people would be transformed, and I could just sit back and enjoy being in a state of bliss!

The last person I saw, in my state of temporary and transitional avatar-hood, was a very miserable, very wealthy real estate developer. He trusted no one, would let himself love no one, would accept very little love from anyone, assumed that all there was in life was money, that he was going to get all of it he could, that he had to watch everybody else so they didn't take it away from him.

In my exalted (temporary) presence, he was transformed, at least temporarily. He was suddenly happy, decided to look at life in a different way, decided to think about other values than money. He started to wonder about changing the way he lived, and perhaps even treating his wife in a loving, human way. He was incredibly grateful for the experience. Unfortunately, one such 50-minute experience was not quite enough, and when I saw him again I was back to my usual state of being. He was waiting for the transformation that he remembered so well to happen again. I couldn't make it happen. He was furious at me despite my explanation that he had experienced a miracle and that somehow I couldn't make the miracle happen more than once.

What had happened was that I started to realize that if I stayed in that state, the Harvey that I knew would not exist anymore, and that terrified me. All the strategies I had worked out all my life to get me to where I was were no longer valid. Parts of me would have to disappear, and a great unknown road was now unveiled before me. I killed the state of bliss. I killed the avatar. I killed the flow of divine love. The experience came back for short periods over one or two months and I have not allowed it to return since. I am in mourning for the loss and I still hope that I will someday soon allow it to return.

Fear and its healing are a favorite subject of mine. I have been afraid all my life. To me, I am the most frightened person I know. In my life I've done more exciting and adventurous things than most people whom I know. This grew out of my first attempt to deal with my fear. To be *counterphobic*, to do the things I was scared of, has led to many, many adventures and many wonderful experiences.

How do you get rid of fear? Are there any things you can do by yourself to decrease or eliminate fear? The main ones are exercise, meditation, breathing, counterphobic behavior, and the healing of traumas.

Exercise can be a major help in the treatment of fear. What is necessary is aerobic exercise. That simply means huffing and puffing for 20 minutes three to four times a week, with a little time before and after for warm up and cool down. Fear is both a psychological and biological experience, and exercise changes your metabolism so that many of the metabolites that give you the exquisitely awful feeling that comes with fear are no longer available. At first the effects may not be dramatic, but with repeated exercise, the level of fear that you live with can be contained. If there are specific outbursts of fear, exercise is a reasonably effective treatment, in much the same way that aspirin can help relieve a headache.

Meditation calms the mind, removing the disturbing effect of large amounts of fear, fear that affects understanding and judgement. Meditation often allows new awareness which can be healing to come to consciousness. There are many, many ways to meditate. Most meditations fail, because they require the meditator to focus his mind. People find that very difficult to do, and unless very strongly motivated, give up meditation after a short period of time. Let me teach you a different kind of meditation, that requires no such focussing of the mind. When you focus your mind, the mind calms, and from that calmness spreads to the rest of the brain and to the body.

In the meditation I am instructing you, the first thing to do is to sit as comfortably as possible. Close your eyes. You can think of anything you want. You can think about your business. You can think about the things you have to do the next day. It really doesn't matter. You can worry if you want to – it really doesn't matter. What you will be trying to do is not to move, and not to swallow.

If you do move, that's no problem – you then simply attempt not to move again, in a non-critical, accepting manner. If a part of your body calls for attention in the form of itching or discomfort, put your mental energy into that part, and sometimes the feeling will disappear. If it does not, simply scratch, or move that part of your body, and then attempt not to move.

Not swallowing seems a little stranger. It's obvious that this meditation should not be done after eating, since the particles of food in your mouth will cause a great deal of saliva to accumulate. It is quite possible not to swallow for long periods of time. If you do swallow, this is not a problem. you simply then attempt *not* to swallow.

Not moving affects the motoric parts of your brain and calms it down. Not swallowing affects your brain stem – the reptilian brain, the most primitive part of our brain, which is responsible for all kinds of body functions. Not swallowing calms that area of your brain. Just as with the more usual kinds of meditation, the calming of the motoric and the brain stem area will spread to the rest of your brain and mind, and will produce most of the effects of other forms of meditation. If you wish, with time, you can add other techniques of meditation, such as imagining you are watching your breath as your belly moves up and down. This form of meditation is both effective and simple.

It is most desirable to meditate for twenty minutes, twice a day. Usually, the best times are said to be in the early morning and the late afternoon. But explore for yourself what seems to work best. If you cannot meditate for twenty minutes twice a day, meditate for twenty minutes once a day. If you cannot meditate for twenty minutes once a day, meditate for ten minutes once a day. Even ten minutes once a day will have an effect. If even ten minutes seems too long, start with shorter periods and slowly start to bring it up to ten minutes, hopefully later bringing it up to twenty minutes.

Don't expect dramatic results immediately. Over a period of time your thinking will be clearer, your fear levels will decrease, your body will be more in a state of peace and relaxation. Think of meditation as not some exotic, far-

Eastern development, but think of it in the same way as your brushing your teeth every day, as part of keeping your mind clean and healthy.

Breathing has been known for thousands of years to be helpful in relieving fear. People who are healthier emotionally and live with less fear have been proven to breathe more deeply than people who are highly neurotic and fear-ridden. There is an entire school of treatment for fear and anxiety and panic states that comes out of Australia, where they do nothing but teach the patients breathing exercises and report very good results.

There is a very simple, very ancient breathing exercise designed to help anyone deepen their level of breathing. With your eyes closed, breathe normally. Then, as you breathe in, count at any rate that naturally comes to your mind. Count to the maximum number that occurs to you from the beginning to the ending of breathing in. It doesn't matter what the number is. If you count fast it will be a higher number, if you count slowly it will be a smaller number. Then add one number to the counting of your normal in breath, so you will be breathing one number deeper. Do that for five to ten minutes each day for about two weeks. As that becomes comfortable, add one more number. Very slowly you are training your body and your mind to live in the presence of slightly deepening breath.

Remember that if you decrease the amount of fear you live with by ten percent, the quality of your life increases one hundred percent.

Music, that most remarkable of all the arts, music that we listen to not only with our ears, but whose vibratory quality approaches the nature of all energy and penetrates through our skin, through our bones, through our tissues, through our organs, *can also reduce fear*. I strongly recommend a piece of rock music called "Force Majeure" by Tangerine Dream, put out in 1979 by Virgin Records. This piece of music emulates and then attempts to heal fear. I have no idea if the artists knew what they were doing, but it is clear to me that this most remarkable piece of music has very healing properties. Listen to this music while breathing slowly and deeply. See the effect it has on your consciousness and on the amount of fear that you live with. If you find other pieces of music that have similar effects for you, I would very much appreciate your writing to me and letting me know.

The counterphobic approach to fear is doing the thing that you are afraid of. It's getting started. Sometimes the fear will evaporate. It certainly is a better approach than obsessing about fear, not moving, and letting moss grow on your ass. It doesn't always work, but it works often enough that it can be useful. Sometimes, if you're lucky, as you push yourself into your fear, it disappears permanently. Often it comes back. That is the limitation of the confrontational, counterphobic approach to fear. If it comes back, and that's your only approach, it means that again and again you have to will yourself to face it. We were not designed to operate indefinitely from a state of will. Will is designed to be an emergency system in the body to force you to do something in a particular situation. But it is so stressful to our minds and to our bodies that if at all possible other more wholesome systems of dealing with stress should be found. As I mentioned, this was my first approach when I started to realize how frightened I was. It led to many, many adventures, and many joys in life. So I can't quite condemn it as at least a partial approach to dealing with fear.

The abreaction, the re-experiencing, the facing of early traumas can also be helpful. There are many ways to do this. An obvious one is to go into therapy with a good therapist and to explore the traumas of your early childhood. Discussing them with a friend, with brothers and sisters, can also be helpful. Interestingly enough, looking at pictures that cover your childhood can very often help you spot times in your life when something traumatic happened. You can see it in your face, in your own face as a baby. Learning to deal with all the emotions surrounding these traumas, sometimes confronting the sources of the trauma directly or in metaphor, facing them courageously, can often be helpful in overcoming fear.

The best psychological definition of fear that I know of was that of Fritz Perls, the founder of Gestalt therapy. Fritz said that fear is your life force, your vitality, corrupted by future fantasies of disaster, of loss, of annihilation, not supported by breathing. What does he mean? What he says suggests several approaches. One is the future fantasies. Fear is not only unreal. It is unreal to the extent that almost everything we are afraid of is our anticipation of something that is happening in the future – that hasn't happened yet, and often never will happen. Finding the future fantasy and looking at it clearly, and realizing that it is a fantasy of the future, not a reality of the present, can very often provide courage, and indeed healing of the fear.

In our society, where accumulation of money is so important, many people are afraid of accumulating wealth. Some of the fears are that, "If I have money, only bad people get money, and then I'll be a bad person and no one will like me, and I don't want to be a bad person anyway, and my parents will reject me and I'll die." Another common one is that "If I become wealthy, people will make demands of me and I'll be drained, so I'm much better off being poor." There are many, many others.

A mother who gave her daughter the message that "you should never be more than me; you must be less than me or I'll withdraw my love," – and for a child the withdrawal of love means abandonment and death, so that there is a death fear – when that young girl becomes a woman and tries to achieve in life, she will most likely sabotage or avoid making her best efforts.

These messages I call the 'Prime Directives.' There are many Prime Directives that are the basis of fear. Prime Directives are conscious, and very often unconscious, inculcated messages that limit, distort and warn us about alleged dangers in our life. For that young woman who was taught that if she was better than her mother she would be killed, that was a very powerful Prime Directive because there is no way a child can survive without its mother and her care and values.

One of mine was "Be the boy I want you to be, not the boy you are," with again the threat of withdrawing of conditional love, and with that loss, the threat of disaster and annihilation.

Prime Directive fears are a major part of the future fantasies of annihilation that Fritz Perls talked about. They are very pervasive in our experience of fear and anxiety. Can you find the Prime Directives – remember, the subtly taught ones are the strongest – that have shaped, limited and added fear to your lives? Make as complete a list as possible. In the simple act of creating the list, in that awareness, the beginning of healing is present.

Annihilation fear is not simply a mental state. Sometimes when I'm working with a patient a strange odor fills the room. It smells to me like sour chow mein, and has also been described as a 'mousy' smell that is very common on psychiatric wards. I call this the smell of annihilation fear. It means to me that in my work with that patient, they have opened up to a level of fear that is very primeval and very primitive and very early, offering the possibility of a very profound level of healing.

You must be willing to risk the illusion of annihilation to move forward in your life, to move through and beyond your fear. **You must be willing to risk the *illusion*, the *illusion*, of annihilation.**

Keeping in touch with the unconscious fantasies that are disturbing your life is one avenue that Fritz Perls suggests for healing your fear. Examine your mind. Examine your background. Talk to and look at the beliefs of your siblings. Examine and pay attention to your dreams. Use any avenue of awareness. Find the mistaken beliefs, the unreal fantasies, the Prime Directives that have distorted your life and filled it with fear.

There is a simple exercise that can not only get you in touch with repressed emotions, but can on occasion help clarify your thinking and awareness. It is called circular breathing.

First breathe normally. Notice that at the end of breathing in and at the end of breathing out, there is a very brief pause. Now eliminate that brief pause at the end of breathing in and the end of breathing out, so the turn around time between inspiration and expiration, expiration and inspiration, happens very rapidly, keeping the breath in between as slow and deep as possible.

Do this for about 3-5 minutes when you are in a state of fear and you have no idea what it's about. Actually during the breathing the necessary information may come to consciousness, sometimes after you return to normal breathing, and sometimes it may be necessary to look at the change of expression in your face caused by the circular breathing. Circular breathing, for reasons that I don't understand, seems to diminish our defenses against awareness of repressed emotions and unconscious ideas and fantasies.

Living in the moment, the Zen aspect of Gestalt therapy, is certainly strongly recommended by Fritz Perls' description of fear and anxiety. There is no past and there is no future. There is only the ongoing present. Observe for yourself that people who seem to be happy live for each moment, enjoy it to the fullest, and are much less concerned about past and future than most of us.

I have had many experiences in my life that confirm this belief. About 25 years ago, I originated the idea that psychological workshops done in the wilderness should be particularly effective. I arranged for a couples encounter group to take place while running the rapids of the Colorado River in the Grand Canyon. In order to enjoy the experience for myself, I limited myself to administration and hired a very capable group leader, Betty Fuller, to handle the therapy side of things. Halfway through the trip, at one of the garden paradises of earth, Havasu Creek, Betty and I shared an adventure.

Havasu Creek is a lovely, clear, iridescent blue stream that flows down from the Grand Canyon Plateau, first coming to a level called the Havasu Plateau, where a tribe of Indians lived in peace for 700 years because no other Indians could find them. It then moves down in a series of waterfalls, through limestone, to the Colorado River, the centre of the Grand Canyon. As it moves through the limestone it creates many small waterfalls and little pools below the waterfalls. The combination of the lovely, clear water and the light colored limestone background makes the water sparkle. It is so clear that every fish can be seen. The water irrigates the land immediately adjacent to it, and at the right time of year produces an incredible garden of radiant wildflowers. Around this centre of limestone are sandstone cliffs covered with cactus that in May have enough moisture to burst into full and dramatic bloom. Just before Havasu Creek empties its clear water into the muddy water of the Colorado River, a natural Romanesque arch spans the river, and sunlight hitting the rippling water creates psychedelic patterns reflected on the ceiling of the Romanesque vaults. As the water enters the Colorado, it mixes in huge swirls of dark brown of the Colorado and light, clear blue of Havasu Creek, creating a giant swirling cookie.

I had decided to walk down the centre of the stream with Betty Fuller. Now you need to know that Betty Fuller is a giant of a woman, looking very much in manner and body build as the ancient queens of Hawaii. She's over six feet tall and very broadly built – a magnificent, powerful woman. We were enjoying walking down the waterfalls, which were only a foot or two high, and through the pools, which were only a foot or two deep, enjoying the beautiful water, the coolness, the flowers around the Havasu Creek and above us the more deserty cactus flowers – until we came to one waterfall that sounded a bit different than the others.

I warned Betty to be cautious because the change in sound sounded a bit ominous. She was ahead of me. In the middle of the stream, which was not very large, was a boulder around which the stream divided into two streamlets. Throwing caution to the winds, Betty looked over the waterfall, which turned out to be about seven or eight feet high, and ended in a deep pool with many rocks.

Her body dammed up the left-hand side of the stream, where she was located. She started to be swept over, tried to grab the rock in the middle in the river, and was only able to grab it with one hand. It swirled her around and she started going over, upside down and backwards, into the waterfall and the rocks below – just as I arrived. I grabbed hold of the arm close to the rock and tried to hold on to the rock as hard as I could. But the force of her body and the water was overwhelming. I was starting to be pulled over, and I had to let her hand go. She disappeared in the thundering rush of the water, as I used all my strength to haul myself up on the rock, thinking, "Oh my God, I've killed Betty Fuller!"

I got up on the rock and Betty was nowhere to be seen. The pool below was not clear. The rush of water had trapped a lot of air, and churned the deep pool below this eight or nine foot waterfall, so nothing could be seen. Betty was not to be seen.

I was debating whether I was agile enough to jump over the rocks and the thundering waterfall into a clearer part of the pool, assuming that she had hit her head and was unconscious and was drowning – when just as I had to make the decision, she surfaced, one hand up in the air holding a sneaker, and shouted, "I know what Fritz Perls meant by the Now!"

The reason that Betty had stayed under the water was that her friend Virginia Satir had lent her the sneakers, and in the traumatic fall a sneaker had come off, and she didn't want to lose Virginia's sneaker!

She had become aware, having studied with and very

successfully treated by Fritz Perls, that as she surrendered to the inevitable power of the water and the waterfall, she had relaxed and experienced no fear. In a way that she had never appreciated before, she knew what Fritz Perls meant by the Now, and that in living in the Now, there was no fear.

Sometimes I am incredibly and foolishly brave. One experience happened when I was an intern at one of the big city hospitals in New York City. We had vast, long wards on which many times the intended number of beds were placed to accommodate the overwhelming flow of sick people that we had to deal with. The ward, which was meant for 45 people, had 90 beds on it. Around each bed were hung pipe racks so that simple white curtains could be drawn to protect patients' privacy and modesty during treatment procedures. Between the rows of bed was a long, narrow corridor through which all the traffic on the ward could move.

One day a black woman was admitted to the hospital with inflammation and pain in her legs that was diagnosed as thrombophlebitis – that is, inflammation of the veins with clotting in the veins. The danger of such a diagnosis was that the clots could break loose and move up into the lungs and heart. The treatment at the time was to elevate the leg, keep it comfortable and warm, and to use anticoagulants so that the blood did not clot excessively.

This was not just any black woman. She had been working cleaning people's houses all her life. She was a giant of a woman, 6'4", built with enormous muscles, her body in the shape of a furniture mover, almost square and tight like a refrigerator.

Her second day on the ward she started singing spirituals. She had a reasonably good voice, and although it was unusual for patients to be singing, we were so busy trying to get our job done and keep a few people alive and healthy, we ignored it. The spirituals continued.

Then, suddenly on the third day, she leaped out of bed.

You must remember, in the hospital they wear these gowns that come on from the front, tie in the back, and hardly protect anybody's modesty, much less that of a huge, muscular woman such as my patient. She charged out of bed, lowered her head and ran up and down the central corridor shouting, "I am a bull! I am a bull!" Everyone fled in terror except one person – me.

At that moment I saw no danger, I saw no fear. I saw only a mad woman charging up and down yelling that she was a bull. Maybe on some level I'd always wanted to be a bull fighter. I gracefully stepped aside while she made her first pass, and on her second pass close to me I jumped on her back, got her in a full Nelson wrestling grip and held her on the ground. Suddenly all the other doctors and staff became brave and ran over to help. And indeed she seemed calmer, and they led her back to bed. It was quiet for a while, about 5 or 10 minutes. In the meantime policemen who were stationed at the hospital started to arrive.

Suddenly she leaped up in bed, grabbed hold of the pipes above the bed and swung her feet out like Tarzan swinging from a branch, and almost decapitated the chief doctor on the ward. With a sudden show of force all the police rushed at her. She calmed down and was immediately placed in a strait jacket to be taken off to a psychiatric hospital.

I don't know how many of you have ever seen a strait jacket. A strait jacket is like a huge sweater with arms twice as long as they should be. It is put on from the front and then the excess fabric that goes beyond the fingertips is wound around to the back where it is tied. A strait jacket is made of incredibly strong canvas fabric. With their arms therefore tied to their back and the jacket firmly over their bodies, it is impossible for anybody to do anything but move their feet.

The patient was calm for a while, then suddenly became agitated again, raised her shoulders, flexed her muscles, and with an incredible display of power and strength, pushed her arms outward and shattered the strait jacket.

For the first time, I became terrified. I realized that if she had wanted to, she could have killed me.

A very similar story happened when I was driving a Triumph sports car on a New England highway. I skidded on some ice, leapt over the centre divider, flew through the air about 6 or 8 feet, landed on my right two wheels, balanced there for a while. The car paused, trying to make up its mind which way it would fall, then fell on all four wheels. I found myself with my car stalled, in the midst of a miraculous break in rush hour traffic.

I quickly got the car started, moved it onto the centre divider, looked around, found there was no damage, and started to drive away – only to find I was shaking so badly after about a quarter of a mile of driving that I could barely control the car.

These are good examples of future projections that happened after the dangerous event. Indeed, I was experiencing 'back to the future' anxiety. Be aware of your leap to the future causing fear. That awareness can help you move toward engaging your life in the moment.

Is Ireland a happy country, a happy culture? Are any Western or modern cultures happy? My answer, and I guess your answer, would be "not very." There have been cultures that I have been fortunate enough to have contact with that are truly happy. The only cultures that are truly happy, in my experience, are cultures that are almost gone now. They are the cultures of the hunter-gatherers. Not all hunter-gatherer cultures are happy, but most happy cultures are hunter-gatherers.

In the modern world, despite our increased sense of security, our increased sense of security does not seem to bring happiness. The socialist countries, which produce the greatest sense of security, are not especially happy. I am particularly knowledgeable about Finland, where a large percentage of men are destructively involved with alcohol. My Finnish friends tell me they think this is due to the fact that the need for the man to protect and provide for his family is gone, so men's indoctrination and training to struggle for those they love is gone, and the meaning to their lives has vanished and they are drowning that loss in alcohol.

In hunter-gatherer cultures, they can only gather enough food to provide for them each day, one at a time. Except for the large overall flow of the seasons, or the migration of the herds, hunter-gatherers live in the moment. It is in the moment where we experience the lack of fear which permits joy and happiness to take place. If a hunter-gatherer has enough food for that day, that is all he can hope for, and he is content. In addition, his life is one of daily struggle to provide the means to sustain himself and his family. As humans beings, we are designed both physically and psychologically to do best and adapt within a certain level of stress and struggle.

The Eskimo (Inuit) culture was the happiest, most neurosis-free culture of any that has ever been developed (to my knowledge). They were a happy people, a loving people. There was very little in the way of competition and struggle. There was almost nothing in the way of hierarchy or authority. There weren't really chieftains; people were placed at the head of the task that they were best at. Sexuality was not a problem. Indeed, families all slept together, and everybody knew everything that was going on. So sex was an easy, comfortable, enjoyable part of their life. There was little in the way of anxiety, depression, psychosis. Survival was too close to the edge. So the culture devised techniques to eliminate this kind of interaction, or to eliminate interpersonal struggles. All energy was needed to get the materials necessary – for food, clothing and shelter.

If you want to experience such a culture, a film by Robert Flaherty, "Nanook of the North," has this delightful and charming young Inuit father going through his daily tasks. In my visit to the Ungava Peninsula, where Nanook lived in the 1920s, I found out that three years after the film was made, the walrus migration didn't happen, and Nanook died of starvation.

In the film "The Gods Must be Crazy," a fantasy, there is a true Bushman, who lives in as much of a hot desert as the Inuit live in a cold desert. The Bushmen also achieved a loving, stress-free, non-hierarchical way of living in the world. The Bushman in the movie is real. His way of behavior, his sweetness, is real. The rest of the movie is a fantasy.

In the United States I lived in an area with people of very modest backgrounds, who struggled very hard and had become financially and professionally successful. Many of them overindulged their children. It was not unusual to se a 15-year-old with a Porsche sports car. Most of these children were unpleasant, arrogant, maladaptive children of an affluent, upwardly mobile society. Many of them as they grew older did very poorly. They were raised to believe that things would be given to them. Many of them lived at the edge of poverty, with handouts from their more successful parents. When I had such a person in treatment I would try to get them in a very open, receptive mood, then ask them to make eye contact with me and say, "Harvey, life is supposed to be difficult." They would respond with incredible tension and writhing in the body, and screams of horror coming from their throats.

One of the ways you can try to stay in the moment and eliminate the disastrous fantasies of the future is to talk about whatever you are afraid of with a therapist, a friend, or any person who will listen receptively and nonjudgementally. For example, when I started writing this book, I was terrified that I couldn't do it. I was absolutely paralysed. I finally couldn't stand the fear that was caused by my panic, and my telling myself that I couldn't write it. I spoke to my wonderful wife, Sarah, and the simple act of telling her, and her sweet laughter of amazement at my self-torture, permitted me to get started. Very rapidly, the fear disappeared, and within minutes the first portion of this work was outlined. Our minds are terrible liars. Telling someone can help us hear the truth and bring us closer to the here and now.

If you can, it is important to sense the border between fear and excitement. Remember, Fritz Perls said that fear is our vitality that has been corrupted. Find something that you have done, or will be doing in your life, that you are looking forward to both with excitement and fear. Think about it a lot, and then play with your mind, play with your thoughts. And almost like in a game of volleyball, move the experience in your mind and body from fear to excitement and back to fear. In this game, perhaps you will learn that fear and excitement are very close to each other, a learning that may be very helpful the next time you experience the fear.

Fear has your life force, your energy, your vitality. So you can't afford to suppress it, to throw it out. It's like a valued friend who is smelly, who needs a bath. It's like gold, which usually comes as an ore with a lot of contaminants, that needs to be refined. It's important to develop a different attitude to fear, not as an enemy, not as something that has to be thrown away or run from, but to welcome fear as much as you possibly can. Whenever you are afraid, start to breathe more deeply. Sometimes, briefly, deeper breathing will increase the awareness of the fear, because the shutting down of the breath is an attempt to numb. Over a period of minutes the fear usually will decrease.

To help you work on your fear, on your transforming it, on your welcoming it in a more organized way, I developed something I call the fear conversion exercise. It is very simple, but it has to be done properly. There are several places that mistakes can be made.

This is best done lying down, but it can be done sitting down. What you attempt to do is to consciously bring up fear. You can bring it up directly, or use any fantasy or event

91

in your life to create the fear in your mind and body. By doing this, you are bringing up your fear. You are taking charge of what happens. The fear is not controlling you. As you bring up this fear, breathe in explosively through your mouth, so that you can feel the cool air at the back of your throat. At the same time, bring up your hands to about to a foot in front of your eyes, as if there was something scary there that you were trying to fend off or push away. Open your eyes as wide as you can. It's a mimicking of the posture of fear, particularly the posture of fear of a young child, a baby, confronted by something that scares it.

It is important when doing this exercise not to stay in the fear position with the eyes open for very long, because that's panic.

Hold the position with the cold air in the back of your throat, your eyes as wide as you can, your hands in front – for about a second or a second and a half. Then relax everything, put your hands back down beside your body, close your eyes, and breathe slowly and deeply until the fear disappears.

Repeat this exercise three times, and perform it on a daily basis. Remember, breathe in explosively so the cold air is in the back of your throat, bring your hands up defensively in front of your eyes. Most people are so afraid of their fear that they won't open their eyes at all. Make sure your eyes are open, forced open as wide as you can. Hold that position for a second and a half, and then relax, breathe deeply and let the breath transform and diminish fear. It is only necessary to do this three times, once a day. Over a period of three to six months, you should notice a considerable diminishing of the amount of fear you live with.

Make friends with your fear. Remember, **your fear is the smelly friend with a good heart. Fear is your tainted gold.**

As an adult, fear is a useless hindrance. What you need is judgement and values. You don't need fear to prevent your crossing the road when the traffic is heavy. You need the judgement that you will be injured. You don't need fear to prevent you from robbing a bank. You need the value that honesty is the way to be in the world, and the judgement that you would probably get caught. Children do not have judgement and values. They need fear to protect them in their lives. Few people ever reach the level of loss of fear, so that they can operate purely out of their values and their judgement. But we can approach this ideal as close as we can. We can survive without fear. Remember, fear is only necessary for children. Fear is a leftover, a childhood legacy that unfortunately persists into adulthood and corrupts and limits and tortures and deteriorates our lives. **Adults need only judgement and values.**

A child cannot in any way control its environment and is therefore very subject to fear. Children are terribly dependent on others, and are therefore very subject to fear. If you want to see how easy it is for a child to be frightened, find a partner who is willing. Both of you remove your shoes. Have your partner lie on the ground with their eyes closed. Gently put one of your feet on their chest, so they can feel your power and their vulnerability. Have them open their eyes, and see how much fear they feel. Then ask them to close their eyes again, and this time put a hateful, rejecting look on your face. Ask them to open their eyes again. Most of the time you'll see the shock in their eyes –and this is only make-believe. Imagine what it is like for a tiny child, totally dependent on its caretakers, its parents.

Some of our susceptibility to fear seems inborn. There are studies that show that there are great differences in children's reactions to a threat. If you take all the children in a newborn nursery, and loudly clap your hands a foot above their heads, some babies will wake up a little upset, cry for a moment, and then go back to sleep. Others will startle, react for long periods of time, scream with muscles tense and color rapidly changing. These are called 'thick-skinned' and 'thin-skinned' children. A thick-skinned child will do very well in a healthy family and will come out in good shape in a very dysfunctional family. A thin-skinned child needs a very sensitive, loving, understanding family. In a traumatic, maladaptive family, they deteriorate.

Fear in adults is the imprint of childhood's excessive vulnerability. The early traumas of childhood that create so much fear are imprints on the consciousness and unconsciousness of the child that are difficult to erase. Any imprint made on a rapidly evolving organism is deeply and primordially engraved. Parents who provide unconditional love, comfort and compassion minimize the amount of childhood fear and therefore the amount of adult fear.

In traditional Eskimo societies, when a child fell and hurt itself in any way, its parents, like all good parents, would pick it up and comfort the child. But instead of tender, compassionate hugging, and soothing, compassionate tones, the Eskimo parents would laugh as they physically comforted the child. They were teaching the child that in periods of trauma and stress, it's important to laugh. The Eskimo, when his snowmobile breaks down on a deteriorating ice floe that could break loose and drift him out to sea, starts to laugh because laughter is more freeing than fears or terror. In that laughter he is able to keep himself free and mobile, to repair his machine, markedly increasing the possibility of saving his life.

There have been cultures without fear. These are the same cultures as the happy cultures. The traditional Inuit or Eskimo culture was almost without fear. There was such tenderness and love on the part of parents, an Eskimo mother carried her child naked against her body, against her skin, also permitting constant, reassuring feelings and fear-negating skin contact for longer periods of time than we permit in our modern societies. This produces children not only with a minimum of fear, but the Inuits, like many such people, had no fear of death. All Western religions are largely based around helping us deal with our fear of death. When the missionaries came to the Inuit, they had a great deal of trouble converting them because what they had to offer was a way to face the fear of death – and the Eskimos had no fear of death. In a town called Pangnirtung, an Inuit community on Baffin Island, several varieties of Protestant religion and Catholic missionaries arrived. They had very little success, although finally the people all became Catholic. Why? The Catholic priest had tea parties with cookies every afternoon, and the people of the community just loved the tea parties and the cookies.

I'd like you to try another unusual visualization that may help you with fear. It involves the brain stem, the reptilian brain, and ancient part of our brain. The brain stem is the upward extension of the spinal cord as it enters the skull. It enters the skull from the spinal column just a short distance in front of the back of the skull, moves upward and forward for about 3-1/2 to 4 inches, and is about as wide as your thumb. Visualize your brain stem in your skull, and have it clearly in your mind's eye. Find some way to arouse fear in your mind and body. Do it any way you can, either directly or with any image of fantasy. And then take your fear from where you usually feel it – in your throat or chest or hands or belly – and move it consciously into your brain stem, and hold the fear in your brain stem. Do this for about three to five minutes.

What did you experience? Some of you may have experienced very little. But a few may feel something unusual, an altered state of consciousness, a little high. Did you feel it? A kind of spiritual or mystical feeling? The brain stem, I have been told by a number of physicists, is the most likely area in the brain that if there is a transducer, a transformer, between our everyday reality and a timeless, spaceless universe, the brain stem is the area. This ancient part of the brain would most likely contain a quantum level centre that could transform information and energy from one reality to another.

Perhaps you might like to try another exercise. In this one, stand gently on your feet, your knees slightly bent, your hands hanging loosely at your sides, your jaw relaxed. With your eyes open, imagine a column of beautiful, golden-white light – white light with specks of scintillating gold in the white – shimmering, glowing, from ceiling to floor. When you can imagine this with your eyes open, imagine it with your eyes closed. Then walk the short distance between that place of imagining and the column of beautiful, shimmering, iridescent, golden-white light. Let that light flood around your body. Let it penetrate every part of you. Stand, with this beautiful light moving through you and around you, for about five minutes. Then step out of the light and open your eyes.

How do you feel? How do you think? Does the world look the same to you? Look for your fear. Can you find it? Does it feel the same? Does it feel as intense?

Fear, my friend,
No growth without you to life's end,
Walk beside my courage to journey's end unknown,
Until an angel comes through wisdom's eye
And heals my heart.

What does that poem say to you? What does it mean to you? Fear is like the blind wise men and the elephant. They all grabbed a different part of the elephant and described the elephant either as its skin, as its tail, as its trunk, as its tusks, as its feet. But what is at the core of the elephant? We are alone and separated, and we feel our insignificance in this world, in this universe. We intuitively feel this. We are children in the world of monsters, real and imagined. We are separated at birth from the universal, from the oneness, so as a child it is easy to be afraid. When we make that spiritual rejoining, and we find that we are part of that oneness – no matter how tentative our awareness of oneness with that universal, fear begins to disappear, **fear disappears**. What is elephant of fear? I believe, from a number of experiences I've had – and hopefully you have had with the last few exercises – that both you and I will know that the elephant of fear is our separation from unity with the universal, from God. Thus the men and women we call saints are able to fearlessly face incredible odds, to perform incredible deeds.

Chapter Four

Depression

Depression is a common problem. As you walk down the street, look at the first 4 people you meet. One of you will come down with a severe, incapacitating depression at some time in their life. In most countries of the world, one in five people succumb to severe depressions. Ask your friends and families if there is anyone among them who has never been depressed. There are very, very few people who are so fortunate never to have tasted the acid of depression. Some depression can be expected as part of all human life. All of us will be depressed at some time, depressions of varying severity, duration and frequency.

Depression feels horrible to depressed people and to those around them. If you have never experienced this, you don't know how debilitating it can be to depressed people, and to the people close to them, to the people who love them.

There is a very simple exercise to demonstrate this fact. Find a partner, and for two minutes put yourself into a depressed frame of mind. Express a continuous stream of depressed thoughts and feelings. Spew out negativity over any aspect of life. Tell all the things that are wrong about you. Tell all the things that are wrong about the world. Tell all the things that are wrong about the other person, if you're feeling brave. Complain about your environment. Complain about the furniture. Complain about the government. Spew forth negativity. Then you can shift and allow your partner to have a turn.

What did it feel like? If you're not feeling absolutely awful, you managed to turn it into a joke. This is the one exercise in this book that I strongly recommend that you do not do. It can spoil your whole day, much less spoil your reading of the rest of the book.

In traditional Eskimo (Inuit) culture, treatment of depression was very interesting. Anyone who became depressed would be strongly supported by the community. Every possible approach – religious, interpersonal – every help and support they could think of would be made available to the depressed person. But after a period of time, depending on whether it was hunting season, or whether there was scarcity of food, the community would decide that they could no longer tolerate the depression. A culture such as the Eskimos', which was a hunter-gatherer culture living at the edge of survival, could not afford negativity in its midst. A person who did not recover from depression would be ejected from the community and forced to live alone, a decision that would mean almost certain death to the depressed person. That may seem cruel, but it was essential. That approach would certainly eliminate all organic depressions. It would also put a dent in most psychological depressions. The ability to tolerate depression in a family and a community is a luxury of abundant, civilized life.

Have you noticed the almost universal phenomenon that when you are depressed, it feels as if it would last forever, but when you're happy you wonder how long it will stay, how long it will last – a very curious, almost universal finding that I have never understood. It certainly implies that depression is stronger than joy, or that depression is more readily tolerated than joy or happiness.

Children under one year old, if not touched or loved, will get into a state that looks very much like depression, from which, as I have already mentioned, their immune systems can break down and many of them will die.

Children of three years old have attempted suicide. I imagine they must have been very intelligent children. There seem to be cycles of mood elevation and depression in all of us. There are long, 6-8 month cycles and, imposed on those, shorter cycles.

Suicide most often is the result of deep despair. Despair is emotional pain of such great severity that there is little hope for any change or relief. When a person loses the little bit of hope that accompanies the despair, surrenders to that despair, no longer fights the despair, what happens? Suicide. Very often at the point when a person is less depressed after being very depressed, they have made a decision to kill themselves – which brings a sense of relief that can often be *misinterpreted* by family and by professionals *that the patient has gotten better*. Sometimes when people surrender to despair, cancer can appear. I was fortunate enough to have in treatment a brilliant civil rights leader, a beloved homosexual priest. He was loved by his parishioners, and was so effective and powerful in his civil rights work that he actually was on Senator Joseph McCarthy's witch hunt persecution list. He was a wonderful man in every way. His life was successful in every way but one. He was a disaster at love. Although in most of his life he surrounded himself with warm, loving, high-minded people, in his homosexual encounters he invariably joined himself with people who were users, betrayers, people who stole his money, people who used him. His love life was one heartbroken experience after another.

He started treatment because of depression secondary to his traumatic love life. Behind the depression was a great deal of despair that traced itself back to his early childhood. He was starting to work on his depression, his despair and his invariable attraction to lovers who were no good for him, when he received a 6-month sabbatical, a paid, six-month leave in gratitude for his years of service, from his parish. He decided to leave the country and to spend his time in the Holy Land. There, he made another liaison that proved to be still another disaster. When he returned, he was noticeably different. He was more comfortable, but the comfort didn't feel wholesome. He no longer was fighting against the depression and the despair.

Within a few months of returning, he developed pains in his stomach. He went to his doctor, who did a series of tests and found nothing wrong. Something told me that things were very wrong. It was almost as if there was a radio station in his stomach broadcasting to me, "Danger! Cancer!" I insisted that he return to his doctor. A repeat of the test confirmed that he had stomach cancer.

Other therapists whom I respect, most notably my friend Virginia Satir, reported very similar experiences when people they were evaluating surrendered to despair and produced a sense about them that something very malignant indeed, that cancer had developed. The diagnosis was made intuitively by the therapist.

Evaluating the suicidal potential of anybody is a very important task, best left to professionals. Very often family and friends are the first line of defense. Never beat around the bush. Ask the person directly. Ask them straight, with eye contact, with no euphemisms. Ask them, "Are you thinking about killing yourself?" Be very open and receptive to their response. Evaluate their tone, the content, all the metacommunications, the aura around the communications, such as body posture, overtones, color of the skin. If they are evasive, push until you get a clear answer. The second question to ask, with the same kind of observation and intensity, is "What are your plans to kill yourself?" If the plans are clear, well thought out, the person certainly is in great danger. If there is a pathological response or any uncertainly, *get professional help immediately.*

Should people have the right to kill themselves? I think it's almost an irrelevant question, because anyone, if they are determined for any length of time, even under close watch in a hospital, will succeed in killing themselves.

Do people have the right to kill themselves? I guess so.

But it really is irrelevant. The wrong people commit suicide. Rotten people rarely commit suicide. Fine, nice people are usually the ones who do. By my definition, if you want to kill yourself, you probably shouldn't. You are a fine, nice human being, and we need you. There are not enough of you on earth.

By and large, people who want to kill themselves are people with superhuman standards and expectations. In addition, people who are depressed and suicidal have disordered thinking and disordered perceptions of reality. They see themselves as hopeless failures or as being terribly bad people. They think that there is no hope, that they never can find love or get over pain, etc., etc., etc. – none of which is true. They deserve a chance to be educated to a more accurate perception of reality. They deserve a chance to have some help humanizing their unreal expectations and standards for themselves. Besides, most suicidal people don't really want to die. They just want to be out of the pain. They just want it to go away for a little while.

I often hear people say that the only reason they don't kill themselves is that they're not brave enough. This is a silly, misguided remark. It has nothing to do with bravery or courage. Suicide has to do with suffering and despair.

Suicide is a variant of murder. At the very least it is murder of the self. People who are considering suicide think they are hurting themselves, but no one else, that everyone else will be better off without them. This is devastatingly untrue. Everyone who cares about or knows a person who commits suicide is deeply damaged by the suicidal event. Sometimes being aware of how damaging suicide would be to loved ones makes it possible for suicidally oriented people to take a more constructive turn in their lives.

One aspect of suicide that suicidal people often overlook is that they are very angry. The anger mostly gets turned against themselves. But although they may be harming themselves, it's an indirect way to hurt, to get back at others.

The most vicious example I've heard of, of the anger that

101

is part of suicide was a suicidal homosexual lover who had been rejected by his partner. In his pain and despair over the rejection, he waited until the rejecting lover went on a ski vacation. He still had keys to the apartment. He went into the empty apartment, took an overdose of pills in the bathtub, and carefully timed his death so that his body would be in an advanced state of decay when his ex-lover returned.

When I was a resident in psychiatry at the Menninger Foundation, I did a research paper on predicting the occurrence of murder by patients who were discharged from mental hospitals. I did a very exhaustive study, and one factor was most predictive of potential murder. Patients who went out and killed somebody after being in a hospital almost invariably had made one or several suicidal attempts while in prison. When the anger that was previously internalised turns outward, suicide can become murder.

Suicide and depression are very close to each other. In the United States, women attempt suicide ten times more frequently than men, but men kill themselves ten times more frequently than women. It's much more serious in the United States when a man threatens suicide. In Ireland men are 4 times more likely to kill themselves than women, while women are 3 times more likely to make suicidal gestures than men. Each person's death threats need to be evaluated individually. Remember that very often hints of suicide, if not manipulative, are basically calls for help from someone who doesn't know any other way to ask for help. It's only if the calls for help are not answered that a fatal attempt will be made.

Male doctors are twice as likely to commit suicide than the average man. Psychiatrists are four times as likely to commit suicide as the average man. (I'm both, but I'm safe – it usually happens when they are under 50. I'm well beyond that, and have nothing to worry about!) Other groups are even higher than psychiatrists. I bet you can't guess which ones. I'll tell you one – ophthalmologists. I am told they are rather a strange breed who have a great deal of trouble with human contact, and prefer to see their patients with a piece of equipment between themselves and their patients.

In my opinion, depression is best not thought of as a disease or illness. Depression should be thought of as a symptom, an expression of disorder with many causes – many, many causes – a complex and difficult problem.

I like to think of mood as something like a temperature thermostat. But instead of heat and cool, we have happiness and well being, or depression.

There are many things that can cause the mood thermostat to dysfunction. There are biological depressions, the best known of which is manic depressive or unipolar depression. People with this thermostat disorder can either be depressed or manicky, manicky being hyperenergetic, not needing sleep, hyperactive, speaking rapidly – in fact being unable to stop speaking – a very high, 'up' mood, but one which doesn't feel pleasant for any length of time and which soon turns to irritability if they are disagreed with. People with this disorder can be either manic or depressed or can move at varying rates of speed and at different times, between manickiness and depression. There is no objective diagnostic test of manic depressive illness. The diagnosis is made by family history of depression, of mood disorders, particularly where there are episodes of mania. Very often accompanying such a history is a spotty history in the family of migraine, alcoholism and attention deficit disorder.

There are as yet no reliable tests for any form of biological depression. A clinician makes this diagnosis based on his clinical evaluation, the history he takes. He mostly looks for the absence of any psychological cause of depression. Many such diagnoses are based on the philosophical approach of many diagnosticians that when in doubt, a depression is biological. One of the problems aside from the fact that there are no biological tests or markers is that it is not very easy to find the psychological causes of depression. Even in people with basic organic or biological depression, psychological factors can precipitate these depressions or intensify them.

Manic depressive illness usually comes on at college age. It can have no emotional cause, or it can be precipitated by emotional trauma, sleep deprivation or by alcohol. People who have manic depressive illness can appear completely normal between episodes, or it can slowly deteriorate into a chronic state of dysfunction. There are variants to manic depressive illness that can appear as unusual behavior or characterological disorder, as in young women who are excessively promiscuous, or young people who become suddenly angry, or have almost what appears like attacks of irresponsibility. Somehow they seem different than other people. With a little experience, you can sense this difference, even though there are no objective, scientific tests.

The usual treatment for manic depressive disorder and its variants is lithium – or antidepressants, although antidepressants sometimes can precipitate manic attacks in people who are depressed. Major tranquilizers are sometimes necessary to suppress the mania, or as the mania evolves into something psychotic.

Did you know that many criminals – something like 30 or more percent of criminals – have abnormal electroencephalograms, that is, brain wave tests. Many suffer from dyslexia. It is subtle and difficult to tease out the interaction between psychology and biology, between behavior and the organic aspects of depression.

One recently recognized cause of depression is now called 'complex partial seizures.' Before that it was called tempero-limbic epilepsy. Before that it was called limbic syndrome. It seems to come on from no known cause, or from birth trauma, or from head injuries in childhood. Almost all children have fallen out of their cribs on their heads, and after a little crying, look all right. But a significant number of them are never right again. The limbic area of the brain is a very important, interconnecting area of the brain that is very poorly protected by the bony and tissue supports of the brain. It is very often injured, and for a long time there don't seem to be any obvious consequences of that injury.

Let me tell you the story of a patient who came to me because she had a history of what seemed to her lifelong depressions. She had received every form of treatment – psychotherapy, drugs, antidepressants. Nothing seemed to help. She asked if I could help her. I asked her the question, "Was there ever a time when she *was* happy and then everything changed?" She replied that everything seemed to go all right until she was seven. I asked her if she could remember exactly what happened, and if there were any injuries. And indeed she had suffered a head injury at the time, with no obvious consequences, except that her life seemed to go differently afterwards, with repeated bouts of depression. Her diagnosis was confirmed by a special form of brain wave exam that was taken after she was deprived of sleep for 24 hours. At that time abnormal electrical spikes appeared in the limbic region of the brain and in an adjacent region called the temporal lobes. The sleep-deprived electro encephalogram (brain wave) test was positive. People who have complex partial seizures often look a bit strange and seem different from other people. They have a history of sudden, angry explosions with little cause, or a history of multiple, vague physical complaints that the doctors can't pin down. Doctors describe patients like this as 'old crocks.' The treatment, just as in epilepsy, is anticonvulsant medication. Limbic area seizure problems affect areas of the brain that are related to emotions, and to many other organ systems and parts of the body.

The range of organic causes of depression seem almost endless. About a year ago, through a whole series of fortuitous circumstances, a woman who seemed to have a clear, psychological depression which brought her to the verge of suicide, proved to have a depression based on copper poisoning in her brain. Depressions related to copper poisoning are becoming more common. Why? There are more and more copper supplements in vitamins, as well as copper plumbing in the home. Most important, as acid rain falls upon mineralized soil around the world, the minerals in the soil are being converted into compounds which will dissolve in water. They then enter the water table and the drinking water. Many people's bodies are not able to eliminate the copper sufficiently, the copper builds up in the body, particularly in the liver and the brain. One of the most significant symptoms of copper poisoning in the brain is depression. Fortunately there is a cure. A drug called penicillinase removes copper from the body.

Food allergies are a controversial source of depression. I have seen experimental films where an apparently normal person took a drink of milk and immediately became severely depressed. Many food substances can cause depression. The most common sources of food allergies are – can you guess? – wheat and chocolate. Anything you have a great longing for and just can't imagine life without, anything that produces that strong a yearning, is likely a food you are allergic to. Sometimes the allergy can take the form of a cerebral allergy and can result in depression. Check your pulse before and after eating such a food. If your pulse rate at rest goes up 5-10 beats per minute, see an allergist.

There are environmental allergies that can cause depression. Some friends of mine gave up psychiatry for a broader field of medicine called alternative and complementary medicine. They had a difficult diagnostic problem. A nun came to them who suffered from severe intermittent depressions. Despite their skills in psychiatry and their skills in medicine, they were utterly puzzled by this depression. But finally, almost by chance, they discovered that whenever the nun prayed too closely over candles, she became severely depressed. She had a cerebral allergy to the hydrocarbons released by the candles.

Switching can cause depression. Switching is a very

poorly understood phenomenon. Its depressive and psychological aspects are something I have stumbled across and have never written about before. Many depressions don't respond to conventional therapy. The phenomenon and concept of switching comes from Chinese medicine through the field of applied kinesiology. One of the signs that a person may be chronically switched is that when they are treated with tricyclic antidepressants, their depressions not only are not helped, they become worse. With the phenomenon of switching, there seems to be poor communication across the corpus callosum, the tissue which connects the two halves of the brain. In Chinese medicine there is said to be an energy flow through channels that the Chinese call meridians. This energy, called 'chi' (pronounced like 'key'), the flow of energy in the meridian channels, is reversed in people who are switched.

It is not in the scope of this writing to discuss switching in detail. But switching is a form of negativity that seems very much like depression. Most of us are switched at some time. Drugs, viruses, and emotional shock cause temporary switching. If you take a person who is chronically switched and stroke their arm gently while thinking loving thoughts and then ask them how it felt, they will reply that it didn't feel good. They didn't like the feeling. If you touch them in the same manner while thinking horrible thoughts about them, they report, "Oh, that feels much better!" Something is reversed. It is as if the ability to taste delicious and spoiled food were reversed.

For therapists who read this book, if you have a session with a patient in which you really feel you're doing a good job, and nothing seems to happen, one of the possibilities is that your patient is at least temporarily switched.

Chronic switching is the real problem. With mild, temporary switching there is obviously some kind of corrective mechanism within our bodies. People who are chronically switched will respond with enthusiastic recognition to the following sentence. Have them repeat it.

"At an early age, I knew that life was so painful that I was only willing to live because I knew I could always die." Chronic switching is the result of early, intense, persistent despair. They are not moving toward the joy of life, but are always looking toward a possible escape through death. They are living life backward. Their life force is focussed backward. That's why negative touch feels ok. They are usually bright, successful in their professional life, but make disastrous marriages, for obvious reasons.

Viruses can cause depression. In fact, mononucleosis is famous for producing chronic depressions. Flu-like illness can result in short-term depressions. Some viruses can become chronic, with endless fatigue and depression. Chronic fatigue syndrome, sometimes called M.E., is an excellent example of this. Very often people who come down with such chronic viral infections have severe, abusive childhoods, became sick with the flu while they were under great emotional stress, and didn't rest when they were ill. It gives them a flu that never goes away. There seem to be cerebral aspects to the viral infection, with memory and concentration problems, and depression. Besides, who wouldn't be depressed if they were always tired?

Psychological depression: Depression means to press down. What is pressed down? Emotions! Repression of emotions is a cause of depression. In psychological depression, emotion is pressed down. Emotion – *e-mote* – means to move out. Emotions are meant to move out, to be expressed. Are Irish people free with their emotions and feelings? No! Depression is often referred to as 'the Irish disease.' Alcohol is not only used to mask fear and anxiety, but to bury depression.

Chronic psychological depression often appears when major belief systems that help sustain and direct our lives break down. I'll give you some examples. A prominent obstetrician came to see me. He was depressed, irritable and critical. The following is almost a direct quotation of how he described himself. "I have a great deal of money. I have a booming practice. I have a huge office building. I have a beautiful home on the water. I have a boat. I have a fancy foreign car, a Ferrari. I have a wife and two children. But I'm not happy." The obvious response to that is, "What has that got to do with being happy?" He was raised by a very successful, materialistic mother, who taught him that if he had the material things of life, he would be happy. Following this map of life had not worked; nothing made sense to him; his depression deepened.

A patient who worked very hard to become president of his corporation believed that success would produce happiness. He ignored his wife and family in his determined, focussed drive to get to the top, only to find that when he got there, success did not produce what he wanted. He became depressed. It is a common belief system that success will produce happiness.

Have you ever heard of the 1930s 'Dancing at Tiffany's, Flying down to Rio' syndrome? Probably not. During the Great Depression of the 1930s, men raised in desperately unhappy homes in the midst of economic hardship managed to get to the cinema. There they saw all the wonderful escapist movies of the '30s. Top hats, dinner jackets with tails, diamonds, dancing ecstatically till dawn. Miserable little Fred saw his path to joy. As an adult he dressed impeccably, wore a $2,000 wristwatch, had lovely paintings on the walls, antiques on the floor, a miserable marriage, depression and alcohol. Movie magic did not transfer itself to real life.

When I was a consultant at the University of Connecticut, I saw a young woman who had been depressed and was starting to break her way out of it. She was a beautiful, brilliant young woman, a University Scholar, the pride of the campus. She had been raised by traditional Jewish parents who wanted their daughter to be a successful professional, a teacher. One day, she left her classroom, walked to the nearest town, found someone sleazy at the bus station, lost her virginity with him, boarded a bus to New York City and took an apartment in Greenwich Village. The belief that she had been raised with was that if she was a good girl and did what her parents wanted, and became the kind of person they wanted her to be, she would have a good life. At 21, she found that this was totally unsatisfactory for her. As her belief system deteriorated, her depression increased. She violently rejected the beliefs that came with her past. Struggling out of the depression, she dramatically changed her life style.

Other examples are when a priest loses his faith. Or a management person who thinks by dint of hard work he can reach the top of the ladder, who finds in his forties or fifties that that's not going to happen. An unusual example was a teenage boy who came from a criminal subculture, where there was a great deal of love in his family. The basic belief of the family was that they were good, everyone else was bad and should be stolen from. He was arrested and sent to a very fine reform school, where he was treated very well. He saw that the people he had been stealing from were fine, caring people. On being incarcerated, he was abandoned by his family as a failed criminal. The belief system that broke down was that his family and his criminal community would always be there for him, and that the rest of the world deserved to be stolen from. The depression that resulted was only resolved when his beliefs about his family and the rest of the world were transformed.

Many women believe that becoming the housewife, the good woman, the loving wife, mother and housekeeper, means they will be loved and taken care of. If that does not happen, I can guarantee you there will be some form of depression. Most of you know someone who fits this dynamic.

These beliefs are part of what I have previously called the *Prime Directives*. Prime Directives are belief systems indoctrinated, often subtly, in childhood. When they break down they frustrate forward movement in life. Our beliefs are the compass that sets the direction of life, the cornerstones on which decisions are made. When they are dysfunctional, depression results. Until our dysfunctional Prime Directives are replaced by new, appropriate beliefs, life founders in apathy, indecision and depression.

I had a mild depression when I was 39 years old, that lasted about two or three years. During that time few people would have noticed my depression, but there were periods of decreased energy, unhappiness, and a lot of thinking about death. I found that by the age of 38 or 39, I had done all the tasks my mother had programmed me to perform. I was to be a successful, busy professional person, not a happy and creative one. I didn't know what to do next. What do I do for an encore? By age 41 or 42, new directions in my life became clear. I would study and create less accepted psychological beliefs and treatments. I discovered the world of the spirit. When that happened, the depression was gone.

When a culture loses its guiding beliefs, the culture becomes depressed. That depression is expressed by individuals in the culture, very often by the young people. The Inuit (Eskimo) culture I can only describe as one of the best adjusted, happiest, most symptom free, un-neurotic societies ever developed on our earth. After World War II they acquired modern technology – rifles, aluminium boats, outboard motors, tundra motor bikes. Instead of peaceful, they became tense. Instead of happy, they became alcoholic and depressed. Instead of cooperation, fighting broke out. Power struggles broke out. The beliefs and values in their lives as hunter-gatherers living at the margins of survival no longer made any sense as they began to deal with grocery stores, formal schooling, and government housing projects – after explosively killing off their food supply in an orgy of hunting made possible by acquired technology.

American Indians can no longer hold the values that came from living in nature and working with the cycles of life. An anthropologist working with Zuni Indians told me that 14-20 percent of all teenage boys committed suicide. They no longer had any meaningful guidelines to direct their lives. Their past was shattered and the present was not yet developed. The chief of a tribe in Colorado wrote to a prominent psychiatrist, pleading, "Please come. My people are dying."

As a culture is going through transformation, as the behaviors and values of the past, as the beliefs of the past are no longer valid, no longer describe and fit the present, the culture dies and in that death depression is rampant. The exceptions to this are rare. The Hopi Indians of Arizona have made the most successful transition into the Western world of any American Indian culture. An ancient culture, many of their beliefs still permitted them to function well in modern life. Among the deterioration of Inuit tribes, occasionally a group has been fortunate enough to be led by a priest who organized the people, taught them new values that fit the new world that was approaching, and so the deterioration and depression did not take place. Do any of you know of a culture in Europe where something like this is happening right now? IRELAND.

As I mentioned previously, the only happy peoples, the only happy cultures, I have ever met are hunter-gatherer cultures. Not all hunter-gatherer cultures are happy, but it is only among this way of life that I have found truly happy people. Why? Hunter-gatherers have to live in the moment. They can only live day by day. Each day the most that they can hope for is to get enough food for that day. When they have found enough food to fill the needs of their people for that day, they are very happy. Hunter-gatherers have few possessions. They are not burdened by possessions. Indeed, they cannot afford to be burdened by possessions because they must move quickly, easily, lightly from place to place. Their desires are simple and limited. Strangely enough, they don't have to work hard. They spend a great deal of their time in individual and group ceremony and socialization.

About 25 years ago an article appeared in Scientific

American magazine about a new group of Aboriginals that had just been discovered in the vast, forbidding, Western Desert of Australia. I glanced at this article when the mail arrived, but had no time to read it because I was putting in a rigorous 10-12 hour per day work load that was necessary to maintain my life style. I remember thinking, "My God, they must have a very difficult time surviving and making a living." later that evening, as I read the article I was astonished to find out that these people, living in this barren, dry desert worked no more than 3-4 hours per day providing their food. The men would go out and hunt the 'prestige' food, an occasional lizard that was the source of their protein. The women, as in most undeveloped cultures, provided most of the calories. They found roots and gathered small nuts from bushes, which were ground up and made into a paste that became their bread. They knew every water hole. If it was a particularly dry season, they just dug the water hole deeper. When it was cold at night they cuddled together and slept with their dogs for warmth. What did they do the rest of the time? They talked, they socialized, they chanted, they danced. I read all this in amazement as I sank, exhausted, into my beautifully crafted, mechanical reclining chair.

In all psychogenic depressions there are suppressed, powerful emotions that rise behind the loss of beliefs, these Prime Directives. We are angry that we were misled. We are frightened into accepting new beliefs, and we are frightened of giving up beliefs. There is pain that these beliefs were foisted on us by those we love. There is sadness at the loss of the beliefs. There is sadness at the loss of faith in those who taught us. Remember, emotion needs to move out, to be expressed. It is important in relieving depression to get in touch with and to discharge these emotions.

Every depression, even a psychological depression, is a biological event. This is most obvious in severe depression, where there is a great decrease in energy, metabolism is measurably lowered, the contraction of the intestines is slowed down, and there are many, many other changes. All thoughts are biological events. Every change in thought, every feeling, changes your biology.

This is easily demonstrated using the 'standing up' exercise on page 12.

What emotions are most commonly depressed in depression? What emotions are hardest to deal with? Pain, anger, fear. With pain we are afraid we will be overwhelmed; with anger that we will kill or be unacceptable; with fear that we will be paralysed, uncomfortable, unable to move.

What other emotions when depressed, when pressed down, can result in depression? Sadness, which always represents a normal, organismic response to any kind of loss – if unacceptable in our consciousness, unacceptable to express, can result in depression. The common fear with sadness is that it will be so overwhelming that you will never emerge from the sadness. Most people use the metaphor of drowning, of being in a pool or a well of sadness, from which they will never emerge.

Many years ago a very prominent local psychotherapist came to see me. He had been suffering from mild depressions all his life, and finally felt it was time to do something about it. We very quickly discovered that he was filled with sadness which he was unaware of. With a simple technique for discharging sadness, which I'll discuss further on, he very rapidly lost his depression and returned to his successful career with greater energy, vitality and happiness.

Much more rare are suppressed and forbidden joy and reverence, or spirituality. People who were punished when they were joyous as a child are very often afraid to express joy as adults. Spiritual or reverential ecstacy and pleasure often violate deeply inculcated intellectual beliefs. But most commonly they are unacceptable because they open the possibility of distinct, even radical, transformation.

Closing of the heart – the depressing, the suppression of love – makes all of us less happy, more irritable, and sour, creating what appears to be depression.

Emotions are bodily expressions of mental states. Without body awareness, there would be no emotions. We need a body to discharge our emotions. If we could take our brain and keep it alive in some way, that brain would have thoughts, but no emotions. A brain that is isolated does not feel. Any culture that devalues the body, the life of the body, the liveness of the body, limits the emotional life and creates the setting for the emergence of depression.

There are many techniques for discharging emotions that have been depressed. Anger can be brought up in the voice, or by hitting an inanimate object such as a pillow or a mattress that we cannot destroy and that we cannot hurt ourselves with. Pain can be discharged through crying; even making believe that you cry can help relieve depression caused by held-down pain. When I lose energy and find myself irritable and depressed, it is most commonly due to pain. I really don't like pain very much, so commonly I keep it out of my awareness, at my own peril. When I no longer can tolerate the depression, and discover that the depression is related to repressed pain, even simply pretending that I'm crying will give me at least temporary relief of my state of low energy.

Fear can be discharged by screaming, a screaming that is best free, without tearing up the vocal cords. Very often our homes are not appropriate places to do this. Sometimes I think cars were invented so that we could get out in the country, roll up all the windows, and make all the noise that we need to make.

The fear conversion exercise described on pp. 90-91 in the Section on Fear and Anxiety is helpful here.

Sadness is discharged through sighing, plaintive, soft sighing. A sadness discharged meditation that I have evolved is very simple to perform and is very valuable if there is a great deal of sadness that needs to be released.

Sit comfortably upright in the back of a dining-style chair. Place your hands palm up on your thighs. Lower your head

115

about 45 degrees and closing your eyes, breathe in and out through your mouth. Breathe out deeply, let breathing in take care of itself. Experiment to see if making sighing sounds deepens the feeling of sadness.

All this posturing is designed to relax the upper chest muscles. When we are repressing sadness, we unconsciously tighten the muscles of the upper part of the chest, which is the area in which sadness is primarily felt in most people's bodies.

Sink into the sadness, like it was a deep pool that you could go deeper and deeper into, a deep well that you could go deeper and deeper into. You are comfortable. You can breathe. Sink into the depths of the sadness until you reach a stopping point. Then end this particular meditation. It may require many repetitions to get enough release.

If you're very lucky, you will discharge all of your sadness, at least temporarily, and find instead – what? Can you guess? – what you will find instead is joy. Joy and sadness are polarities of the same experience. If we are trapped in our sadness, we cannot fully experience our joy. If we release the sadness, joy can flood through us, a joy which will erupt spontaneously with no particular reason for being there.

If you're depressed, even a little depressed, there is a very simple exercise to help you identify which emotions are the ones causing the trouble, which emotions are being held down.

You simply say out loud, "I don't want to feel my _____" and serially insert each emotion. Listen in your body-mind, in all parts of yourself, for any kind of response that says yes or no. You'll be saying, "I don't want to feel my fear." Then listen. Be aware. "I don't want to feel my anger." "I don't want to feel my pain." "I don't want to feel my sadness." "I don't want to feel my love." "I don't want to feel my joy." "I don't want to feel my sexual feelings." "I don't want to feel my reverence." (Reverence is the feeling that one would have in a great cathedral, or in the presence

116

of a grove of giant, ancient trees.)

Another way of getting in touch with repressed feelings and occasionally with thoughts is called circular breathing. I described circular breathing in the section about Fear and Anxiety. You may not actually be able to sense the shift in emotion produced by this technique, but a quick glance in a mirror at the end of circular breathing may show you a look or fear, or sadness, or anger on your face that you are not sufficiently in touch with to pick up while scanning your own body.

Let me now teach you a very useful meditation on all emotions that can easily be done by anybody in their home, with a tape recorder.

The first step is to record instructions to yourself on the tape recorder. I have discovered that instructions given by anybody else during this meditation are not nearly as effective as hearing your own voice lead you through the meditation. It is important to do it on a tape, because having to remember each step in the meditation, rather than listening to the instructions, allows us to put too much of our consciousness into memory and intellect, spoiling the purpose of the meditation. The purpose is to discharge emotions – to open the channels of clogged emotions, to free the moving out of all the range of emotions that are necessary for our emotional, and indeed for our physical health.

Patients have reported that this exercise not only improves people's mental health and relieves depression, but has also been known to improve and promote healing of psychosomatic illnesses.

In preparing the tape, serially go through each emotion that I will list below. After you announce a particular emotion, have some object with which you can make a neutral sound, such as a tapping sound on a table, or hitting a not-too-musical or resonant glass with a fork or a knife.

Each time a sound is heard after the emotion is announced, you will attempt to feel that emotion. You can feel it directly, or create the image of a situation that evoked

117

that emotion. In addition, the fingertips of your non-dominant hand are to be placed just above your knee, at the top of your knee where the bone ends, in the soft area just beyond the bone. It is acceptable to rest your forearm and elbow on the arms of a chair, but your hand should not rest on your thigh. Only the fingertips of your non-dominant hand should rest on the soft area just above the bony cap of your knee.

As you are feeling each emotion following each sound cue, briefly press into the soft area above your knee, in a pattern that evokes the feeling of that emotion. Anger would be a deep, fairly sharp pressure. Joy would be a light, intermittent kind of pressure. The only emotion that I will list that cannot be expressed by a downward, outward pressure of your fingers is fear. For that it will be necessary to dig into the soft part above your kneecap and pull toward the trunk of your body. Remember, fear is a moving away kinetically rather than a moving out. All other emotions can be manually expressed into the area above your kneecap by a downward, outward motion.

Recreate each emotion episodically for three to five minutes. Allow the tapping that announces that the emotion is to be experienced to occur at random intervals from 5 to a maximum of 15 seconds apart. If the instruction to feel the emotion is done rhythmically, a hypnotic state sets in which will not permit the discharge of emotions.

Carry out this meditation in a darkened, quiet room. Always allow enough time so that you complete the range of emotions. It is not useful, in fact might be harmful, to do the more unpleasant emotions without finishing with the more positive and uplifting emotions.

The first emotion to be felt and expressed with your fingertips in the soft spot above your kneecap is ANXIETY. The second emotion is FEAR. The third emotion is ANGER. The fourth emotion is PAIN, emotional pain. The fifth emotion is SADNESS. The sixth emotion is LOVE. The seventh emotion is JOY. The eighth emotion is SEXUAL

FEELINGS. The ninth emotion is PEACE. The tenth emotion is REVERENCE or AWE.

The total time to do this meditation is about 45-50 minutes. Once or twice a week maximum is all that is necessary to get the desired result. Try this meditation over a period of three months to a year and observe its effect on your physical and mental health.

WARNING: On occasion, very powerful and distressing repressed emotions may suddenly flood through and cause great discomfort. If this happens and they are not readily dealt with, consult an experienced therapist who knows how to deal with emotions, and who can support you through a healing experience with that particular emotion. This does not mean that anything bad has happened. It simply means that an extremely uncomfortable but necessary opening has occurred.

Chapter Five

Getting Stuck on the Healing Road, and Spiritual Aspects of Mental Health

Life can be viewed as a road, a path, a circle, or a spiral. If you believe in reincarnation, the circle of life becomes a spiral. We are all on the same journey. I believe it to be a journey of learning – learning what is real, unreal, true, not true – a journey toward wisdom. Wisdom is understanding the nature of things, of truth, of reality. This life, this world, is a school where, if we do not learn the lessons of life, they are repeated and repeated with increasing vigor and severity.

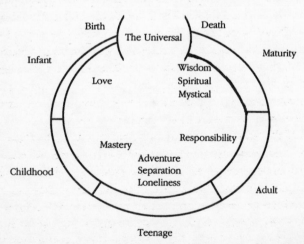

I like to divide life into five stages: infant, child, teenager, adult, and maturity. These are stages of life where blocks can occur.

The task of infancy is learning about love. The task of childhood is learning about mastery. The tasks of the teenager are separation, dealing with loneliness, and adventure. The task of the adult is responsibility, carrying on the work of the world. The tasks of maturity are wisdom, and spiritual and mystical evolvement.

For the child, its mother, its parents, its family, are the world. They are the teachers who teach us who we are, and the nature of the world. They teach us in varying degrees of accuracy or inaccuracy. We learn as a child how to maximize the 'goodies' of the world coming to us – attention, love, things – and to avoid the dangers of the world, such as pain and annihilation.

Children are dependent totally for their survival on their parents. The threat of death is never far away – not only physical abandonment represents death to a child, but the loss of love to an infant equals abandonment, equals death. Broader than death is annihilation. Humiliation, shame, embarrassment, denigration, are all forms of annihilation, as well as physical death. These are little deaths, little murders.

These teachings, these learnings, become innate, intuitive, automatic. As they are precipitated around our core, they become our character. Character is the congealing of early teachings around our core, the adaptive patterns constructed from these early teachings and experiences. Experience is the greatest teacher.

If the teachings about our nature and that of the world are accurate, our character (adaptive patterns) moves us through the stages of life. If the teachings about our nature and the nature of the world, of reality, are maladaptive, then problems develop in the stages of life, and WE ARE STUCK. We then cannot move easily and fully through that stage. Therefore, YOU ARE NOT MENTALLY OR EMOTIONALLY ILL, YOU ARE STUCK. Stuck because of old, erroneous messages, 'tapes,' learnings, that are maladaptive. Stuck because these maladaptive learnings from our primary teachers (the family) make our natural emotional expressions, our natural yearnings, our natural growth patterns and directions unacceptable and unattainable. We lose our way, and only learn this when we find ourselves stuck in one of the stages of life, and develop symptoms of our "stuckness." – discomfort, depression, anxiety, frustration, agitation. When we are stuck we are unequipped to move through that stage smoothly and comfortably, and therefore are poorly prepared for the next stage of life which inevitably, in time, makes its appearance.

The fear of loss or of annihilation is behind all maladaptive behavior, all neurosis, all "stuckness," all character flaws. Therefore, there is great terror in giving up these maladaptive learnings. You have to give up these maladaptive learnings. You have to replace these maladaptive learnings to move on, to get "un-stuck." Remember, you must be willing to move through the ILLUSION of the valley of the shadow of annihilation and loss to unlearn and relearn. **You must be willing to move through the ILLUSION of the valley of the shadow of annihilation and loss to unlearn and relearn.** So change and growth seem fearful and therefore difficult to accomplish. So we often stay stuck.

These potent learnings, these 'Prime Directives,' are powerful messages that pervade all of life, all of character. Examples of Prime Directives are: "I want only your good. Therefore, how can you disbelieve or disagree with me? If you follow my teachings, all will be well. If you do not, you will be destroyed. You are worthless." Prime Directive: "Everyone knows better than you." Prime Directive: "If you succeed and do better than me, you will be abandoned and destroyed." Prime Directive (common in spoiled, wealthy areas of America – I have called it the 'Fairfield County Syndrome'): "All the things of life will come to you. You won't have to earn or struggle for them." Prime Directive:

"You are not wanted. You had no reason to be born. You're a boy and you should have been a girl. You're a girl and you should have been a boy." Prime Directive: "Die. Get sick. You are a bad and sinful, unworthy person."

Prime Directive: "You were placed on this earth to make me happy" – a very common Prime Directive in unhappy marriages. A child cannot make a parent happy. No person can make another person happy. A small child cannot be responsible for an older. large person's happiness. This impossibility results in guilt, a sense of failure, destroying the evolving child's life in an attempt to make others happy.

Prime Directive: "If you move boldly in the world you will be destroyed. Be cautious. Take few, or small steps. There are Tyrannosaurus Rexes everywhere." Prime Directive: "There is always something to worry about." Prime Directive: "Money is success." Prime Directive: "Be shy and introverted to be acceptable."

What are *your* Prime Directives? Have you come up with any since I first mentioned them earlier in this writing? It's much easier to spot them in someone close to you, most easy in someone not close to you, hardest to identify in yourself. If you're having trouble finding your own Prime Directives, look for them in the people around you. The practice will be useful.

There are, of course, Prime Directives that successfully describe reality and the world, but many do not. Where do these Prime Directives get you? They have gotten you stuck. Remember, these maladaptive learnings are usually out of awareness, or if in awareness, are profoundly believed.

I asked a patient of mine to lie back on a sofa, reach out her hands as if she were a child, imagining herself to be a small infant, and to see the faces of her parents above her, and to each parent sequentially to say, "You're so lucky to have me!" She could not utter a word. She could not get these words out of her mouth. Even as an exercise, even as a role, she could not utter these words. Can you imagine the information she was given about herself and her worth? Can you imagine that this has caused difficulty in many phases of her life?

It's easy to see, using this model, where and how you get stuck. If there was no love, or distorted love as a child, not enough touching, if severe enough, you could become depressed, even ill, or die in childhood. Learning love is the most basic of all learnings. If you are taught that you are lovable only if you submit to me, the parent, if you please me, the parent, this produces in marriages women with long-suffering relationships in which love is never returned or rewarded.

If the defect of learning comes at the age of mastery, if you are told, "you are clumsy, you can't do anything, you make mistakes, making mistakes is dangerous. You have to be perfect," you will become stuck in childhood without the self-confidence that you can do things, resulting in trouble at maturity.

Learning as a teenager that the world is dangerous, teaching you that only if you stay stuck, glued to your parents can you prosper and survive, produces fear of taking risks, of separation – and a distorted ability to approach mature love and accomplishment.

Your culture helps determine where you get stuck. The chronically unemployed underclass, who are always on the dole, who have never seen any member of the family support themselves, learn few if any mastering skills. This makes it very hard for them to take on the responsibilities and tasks of adult life. Girls play with dolls, boys with toys that need construction and that do things. Therefore girls have problems in mastery of many adult skills which require the handling and manipulation of objects.

If you have been told as a child, "You never were as good as I am, the parent, never be more successful than I am," as an adult you are very limited in your career choices. You may very well become a loser.

You are not going to be able to move through the stage of maturity if money and power are your only values. You are not going to be able to move through the stage of maturity if you were raised narcissistically, to believe that you are the centre of the universe. Narcissism is caused by extreme and fawning conditional love that tells you the lie that you are at the centre of all things, while at the same time you intuitively know that this is not true. This causes a great quivering of insecurity, covered by the glittering mirror of narcissism. If you are the centre of the universe in your narcissism, how can you surrender to the universal?

In India a recognition of the tasks of maturity is part of the culture. In his middle to late fifties, a successful Indian businessman may turn his business over to his children, and spend 5-10 years at an ashram learning to develop his spiritual and mystical nature. Nobody thinks this is very strange. This is considered a normal, healthy and desirable part of life. After a period of time, he returns to his family, probably only partially rekindling his involvement in his business. If that happened here, what would people say? What would people think? Would it be accepted? What happens here instead is alcoholism, depression, promiscuity, workaholism – all the things that we call 'mid-life crisis.'

Bob, the merchant, came to see me complaining of unhappiness, of depression. "I think all the time," he said, "that my business is going bad. I think all the time about money. I yell at my wife for spending on our credit card even after I told her that it was ok. I'm becoming just like my father, who had the business before me, and it killed him." I gave him the following sentence: "I am too tied down to the material side of life. I'm going to open up my spiritual side." He started to glow, a golden glow, and his depression vanished. The lines on his face softened. The greyness was replaced with pink.

Inherited aspects of your character, parameters such as whether you're high-strung or phlegmatic at birth, the strength of your life force, and good or bad fortune, help to determine how badly you are stuck. Remember, not everybody is born into this world the same.

I have had a friend who is half Hawaiian, one quarter Black and one quarter Cherokee Indian. He grew up in the slums of Harlem, where he was a thief, a murderer and a gang leader. He ended up in a boys' correctional institution, where a nun saw his inner beauty, stayed close to him and made it possible for him to move out of the degradation and distortion of the ghetto to become a college graduate and a psychiatric social worker. Not every Harlem resident has such good fortune.

If you are stuck at any part of life's journey, it will distort the rest of the path, the rest of the cycle. Family loyalty, loyalty to those we love, no matter how badly they have treated us, loyalty to their beliefs, is part of our stuckness. We have to symbolically 'de-parent' our parents, to eliminate their roles as parents and accept them as people, accept them as Noreen and Brian, not as Mommy and Daddy. Remember, even if you don't believe it, you cannot help loving your parents. That love can produce a perverted sense of loyalty to their teachings. We must abandon those teachings that are dysfunctional and cause us to get stuck in the journey of life.

Saint Francis was born into a wealthy, middle-class family, raised with the best food, clothing and education that his times could buy. After a traumatic experience as a prisoner of war, he returned home, ill and transformed. One day he took all his father's wealth that he could put his hands on and threw it out the window to the poor people in the streets below. His father was enraged; he dragged his son to the cathedral and summoned the bishop.

On the steps of the cathedral he ranted, "My son has thrown away my wealth. Why has he done this to me? What can you do about it? I've given him everything – the best food, the best education." Saint Francis replied, "Father, I was only trying to help you. You are burdened, you are imprisoned by your wealth. I was trying to free you." His father was even more enraged, and added that the very fine clothes on his son's back came from his indulgent father.

Saint Francis is said to have carefully removed his clothing, until he stood naked on the steps of the cathedral before his father, before the bishop, before all the assembled people of the town, folded his clothing and handed it to his father, saying, "There are no more fathers, and there are no more sons."

Saint Francis was saying, "I am no longer loyal to your misteachings."

The fear involved in stuckness is not just of loss and annihilation, but fear of the unformed place, the amorphous place in all transitions where we no longer are what we were and we are not yet what we will become. This must be an accepted part of all transitions, changes, relearnings and transformations. If you will not tolerate the unformed place, you cannot change and you will remain stuck.

Our fear is a fear of mental health, fear of all we already are and need to free up. We are like Michelangelo's sculptures. Michelangelo is reported to have said that he did not create his sculptures, he merely freed up the sculpture that was already in the stone. He removed the excess. He removed the unnecessary parts. In each of us is that perfect Michelangelo sculpture. It's already there. It needs to be freed of the excess – the distorted learnings and beliefs, the repressed emotions, the untruths that imprison the inner perfection and beauty.

A most pernicious fear is the fear of mental health. All maladaptive learnings produce this fear. Therefore the problem is not mental illness, but the fear of mental health. **The problem is not mental illness, but the fear of mental health.** This is what limits many psychotherapies and psychotherapists. They focus on psychopathology and not enough on the fear of mental health. We are afraid to free the Michelangelo statue in us. Mental health is being alive, vital, vigorous, happy, able to express emotions, not anchored in fear, ignorance or misshapen learnings, with a sparkle in the eye – free to explore life, free to become all we are born to be. Mental health is knowing what you want, what you feel, what you believe. Mental health is accepting your autonomy, your responsibility for yourself, standing on your own two feet.

Would you like to become a healer of others? I hope your answer was yes. We need you. At least a quarter to half the population of the world have to be healers in order to heal the population of our planet. The philosopher Pascal has said, "All the world is a hospital and all of us are patients in it." To which I would add that an occasional patient wears a special hat and calls himself a doctor.

To become a healer, the first and most important step is to see in the other the perfection that at some level they already are. Never lose sight of this, no matter how the other person responds or behaves. Do not let them confuse or deflect your vision. People are afraid to see themselves as perfect, because they intuitively know it will transform them. They will try to get you to back down. The golden centre is what we already are, without irrational fears and distorted learning. Look around you where you are. Look around you as you walk in the street. See the golden centre in everyone. You remember the exercise earlier in this book in which you chose a partner and alternately saw the golden centre in each other. Try it again now and see if there is any difference, if it is in any way more intense. See any imperfections as the rubble that needs to be cleared away from that centre. See the perfection. See the golden centre. Hold that vision despite any negative behavior and attitudes, any signs of mislearning or stuckness. If you persist despite their best efforts to stop you, at first they will resist you, and then they will start to see their own golden centre and become un-stuck – or they will leave. Mother Teresa is so effective because she sees this even in the lowest, most degraded human being.

A patient of mine was a director of a Protestant group's relief efforts in southeast Asia. He saw so much suffering and misery that he returned to the United States depressed, with a depression that it took him many months to recover from. He decided that something had to change in him if he was to continue his charitable work. He knew that Mother Teresa was a tough, vibrant old lady who had seen and in her own hands soothed the suffering of poor, uneducated, plodding, diseased humans. Somehow she had not allowed herself to be brought down, as he had. He went to India and spoke to Mother Teresa, and talked to her about his problem. Her reply was, "You must have faith and believe in Jesus." He was very disappointed, and desperately pleaded, "I know all that stuff. It's no help whatsoever." She suddenly turned to him and, with gentleness in her voice and eyes, said, "You must love the beauty in each human being. You must love them one by one."

Remember, man is a moral creature, and can only do evil if he can fool himself into thinking that it is moral. Otherwise, no man can lift his arm to strike an evil blow. To do evil you must see the other as bad or sub-human. At Wounded Knee, in the United States, the U.S. Cavalry rode in to a peaceful Indian village, shot and killed every man, woman and child, and crushed the heads of babies with the butts of their rifles. They believed that Indians were not human. They believed that our American Indians were like vermin to be exterminated.

Do you know the difference between a good person and a bad person? A bad person does bad things, knows he is doing bad things, and doesn't care. A good person must do bad things by fooling himself that the other person deserves them, or by fooling himself that he's not doing anything bad at all. Once a good person finds out that what he is doing is destructive, he feels remorseful, and will change. Good people and bad people do bad things.

People will stay mired down in the misery of their stuckness not because they like it – no one enjoys misery, no one enjoys stuckness. They will accept the misery of their stuckness out of fear of annihilation, out of fear of change, out of fear of mental health.

Let me tell you the story of Tony. Tony has an

enormously warm and generous heart. Tony has a mind with the fastest brain-computer I have ever known. Tony is an officer of a well-known multinational corporation. I don't think that Tony graduated from anything higher than high school, but achieved his corporate position through sheer brilliance. As I tell you the story of Tony, see if you can guess where he is stuck, where were his traumas and what were his mis-teachings.

Tony was born into a lower class Greek family that inhabited an ethnic enclave in Brooklyn. No one in his family was ever educated. His father, who is clearly as brilliant as Tony, worked all his live as a humble taxi driver. There was very little support, particularly emotional support, in Tony's family. Particularly lacking in emotional tenderness and warmth was Tony's mother. Tony helped raise himself in a busy family, surrounded by numerous relatives. The family was afraid of education and success. Education and success meant to them the ending of the family, a family that would fragment and move away. The only avenue toward success that was ever encouraged or admired was an uncle who managed to own and train a horse that won the Kentucky Derby. He was the family hero. Betting on the races was a constant preoccupation of the family. Success in betting on the races was a source of great pride.

Although Tony was an extremely loving and generous man, it took a while to appreciate this side of him. He easily showed his lightning-rapid intelligence, but his emotions were muted, until, with time, you understood that he was caring and generous. Tony would give you the shirt off his back. If you needed a friend, Tony would be there.

Tony hated his work. Every day on his way to work, he was filled with dread and suffered severe anxiety attacks. He thought he was fainting, dying, that something terrible was happening to him. He suffered from fear of flying, a fear that caused him to invent elaborate excuses as to why he couldn't carry out his corporate duties by air.

Tony's anxiety spread beyond his work. Anxiety attacks,

130

with sweating and disorientation, could occur anytime during the day and often during the night. Tony married an incredibly beautiful woman, selfish, with a heart of stone, who gave him no love and no warmth.

Having been raised in the nether regions of New York, Tony had 'street smarts' and a crafty cunning that made it easy for him to move near the boundaries of legality. These traits plus an incredible ability to see possibilities, to negotiate deals, made Tony the ideal entrepreneur. But Tony worked as an officer in the army we call a corporation. Every day he went to work dreading the day. He was bored to the point of insanity. He was able to do his work in anywhere from five minutes to one hour. He could not stand the corporate posturings and self-protection, when the issues and solutions were instantly available to him. He could barely control shouting obscenities during long, drawn out corporate decision-making meetings.

What did he do with his time? In the privacy of his office Tony handicapped the horse races. How many people do you know who have won through betting on horse races up to $250,000 per year? Friends of mine have seen him coming home from the race track with a shopping bag filled with money. Of course, the next day he might lose $5,000-10,000 betting, but that was all part of the game, nothing to be overly concerned about.

Tony would never be happy in his work unless he ran the show, unless he was the boss who could make rapid fire decisions in his own company. Tony needed to be a president and entrepreneur. A ready source of capital to back him in this undertaking flowed through his fingers. But Tony was intermittently broke or in great debt. How did he manage this? He managed this by his fervent desire to buy a reasonably priced race horse and develop it to be a major Derby winner. Raising and developing and training horses is an extremely expensive hobby – especially horses that frequently pull muscles or tendons, break their legs and develop illnesses. Tony was constantly bankrupting himself with a stable of horses.

When he was deeply in the hole financially, Tony would suddenly become focussed, go to the track and, within a period of days to weeks, recoup the large sum of money that he had lost. Sometimes he would put together an extracurricular investment deal, and again recoup the huge debt he had gotten himself into. In order to finance a horse purchase, he had mortgaged his house. The horse, as usual, was a disaster. Tony said, "There's no way that bank is going to take my house." Within six weeks, he walked into the bank and paid off his huge debt in cash.

Tony had trapped himself in an incredible cycle of highs and lows, whose excitement was as addicting to him as heroin is to a junkie. What would he do without his 'fix'? I never found out, for it never happened. I suspect that his first reaction would have been depression.

Tony was clearly stuck in the adult part of his life. The low self esteem that came from the lack of love and support, especially by his mother, affected both his poor choice of mate and his inability to find the courage to become his own boss. The terror of the threat of abandonment via education or getting ahead clearly dictated many of the choices he made in life. He went as far as he could, before the inborn terror limited his choices and movement. His family were fascinated by his struggles at the track, but never mentioned once that he had achieved a high position in a major corporation.

If someone moves to reality and clarity, if someone becomes un-stuck, then they have the energy and freedom to go on in life. All growth, psychological, spiritual, emotional, even economic, leads in one direction – to complete the cycle. If you get to know people very well, almost everybody will say that they want to be wealthy, but if you listen to them carefully and watch their behavior, you will see that most people are afraid of wealth and abundance – afraid that they don't deserve it, afraid they will be abandoned if they get it, afraid that it means that they're bad, afraid that it means that no one will take care of them.

When we are no longer stuck and are completing each phase in the cycle of life, we are free to ask the important questions of life. Free movement in the cycle frees us from our stuckness – frees us to ask, "What is life all about?" The minute you ask the meaning of life, the minute you ask what is life all about, you have become, inevitably, a spiritual seeker.

Where do we all go, as we move freely in the circle of life? We go to death. If you move freely in that circle, you inevitably ask, "Is there anything after death" – or, "Is there anything before death?" "What is it all about? Why is there suffering? What is truth? What is universal and eternal?" – You have become a seeker on the spiritual journey.

Remember: all human growth and learning is spiritual. All human growth and learning moves us toward spirituality. Anywhere there is distortion, unreality, in a human being, there is a blocked point and a stuck point. It doesn't matter if it is material, intellectual, emotional or spiritual. All growth tends to move us in a spiritual direction. Carl Jung said, "Every psychological problem over forty is a spiritual issue."

Mike was an Episcopal priest. He was a deeply pious, spiritual man with a constricted and controlled personality that made him admirable, but slightly boring. Mike had a marriage of less than desirable quality, but he was very emotionally dependent on his wife. His wife became tired of his dependency and sought treatment for herself. As she separated the abnormal closeness between them, her husband, Mike, started to develop anxiety attacks and came to see me to help heal this distress.

His treatment was like nothing I had ever experienced before. Everything I did, every opening in experience I encouraged him to have, resulted in the most incredible mystical and spiritual experiences, some so amazing and unbelievable that I am very hesitant to write to you about them. Mike became lively and fascinating. He developed unusual abilities. He could tell what people were thinking and feeling, without them saying a word to him. I myself checked his ability to see strangers at a distance who were described to him, and then, without any information, to be able to report what they were doing and what they were wearing at that moment. Every night, Mike experienced himself leaving his body and being taken by entities to a school where a very vigorous re-education was taking place. He was stunned and amazed and excited by all these occurrences, and very pleased that his bishop, far from being questioning or derogatory, was very supportive of his amazing transformation.

At the same time, a young, attractive female divinity student became an intern in his church. They fell in love. Each knew of the love of the other, but each, in their caution, permitted nothing unusual or physical to happen.

After about a year of this remarkable transformation in his life, Mike made two significant decisions. One: he decided not to pursue his love, and to stay with his wife. Two: Mike could no longer tolerate the amazing experiences he was having. It violated every conservative bone in his body, and Mike shut down his unique mystical journey. He once more became a pleasant, somewhat dull, but fine clergyman who, within three months said to me after visiting a family cemetery, "I hear my ancestors calling me." Within four months he had developed stomach pain. Within five months he was diagnosed as having inoperable pancreatic cancer. Within a year Mike was dead. During that year I did everything I could to find alternative forms of treatment for Mike. But Mike managed never to do anything about them. Mike was ready to die. It is my belief that in making the two monumental decisions, to limit the love in his life and to limit his mystical journey, Mike had already chosen death.

A hard-driving, womanizing, middle-management, alcoholic businessman, a member of a large, multinational corporation, in his middle fifties had a heart attack, died, and experienced himself leaving his body, going through a tunnel of light, and finding dead relatives and divine beings at the end of the tunnel. He was told that he had to return to earth – where he terminated his corporate position and entered divinity school. He is now a practicing Protestant minister. I have had two patients, one relative and one acquaintance with very similar kinds of experience.

Spiritual, to me, is a place inside that feels like home. You feel at peace, and you feel benevolent to all living creatures. You know that you are a part of something much larger than yourself. Mysticism is becoming aware that there is more to reality than our five senses teach us.

You might want to repeat the golden centre shuttling exercise and the column of gold light now. See if the experience is in any way different to the previous time you practiced them.

Would you like to take a further, if temporary, step in the spiritual part of your journey? If the answer is yes, I have an interesting exercise for you.

First find a quiet place with a chair. In that chair, in your mind, place somebody that you are very angry with – hateful, if possible. As loudly and vituperatively as possible, direct a stream of vicious, venomous negativity at the object of your contempt and distaste.

Now separate yourself from that experience. Sit in a fairly erect, comfortable chair and do the following. (It is necessary for me to teach you this in several stages. Although the exercise is not complicated, it can be confusing.) The first thing to do is to breathe in fully, in a jerky, staccato manner. At the end of the in-breath, hold your breath for a moment, and then breathe out in a staccato, jerky manner.

Now that you have accomplished this part of the exercise, add the following: As you breathe in, tighten up your pelvic floor, that is your anus area in men and your vagina and anus area in women – And tighten up your abdomen as tight as you can, as you are breathing in in a staccato, jerky manner. Then hold your breath for an instant, as before, and breathe out in a staccato, jerky manner. With the breathing out, push down your pelvic floor and push out your abdomen.

Once you have the knack of this, do three cycles of this breathing. Wait a moment when you are finished (you may be a little woozy), and then once again stand up. Approach the chair of your vituperation, and let loose again.

Any difference this time? You may be having trouble getting the very words out of your mouth. You probably will be having trouble feeling the internal rise of negativity and wrath in your body. If you do manage to get the words out, I'd be surprised if there was any real feeling or emotional content, any music to accompany the words.

What has happened? A miracle has taken place! You did a simple breathing exercise and it's impossible for you to express any negativity. Try expressing benevolent thoughts, loving thoughts. I don't think you'll find any difficulty. It's a miracle, but don't worry, it won't last! Within 10 to 30 minutes of this transformation, you will return to normal.

Spiritual freedom or the lack of it, like all emotional and characterological aspects of our personality, is encoded in the body and in body tensions. Spirituality is an energy affected by thought and by muscular tension. In each of us is a saint held in prison by erroneous thoughts and resultant muscular tensions. **In each of us is a saint held in prison.**

EPILOGUE

In the past, the long-distant past, Ireland has had a primary place in the spiritual and mystical journey of mankind. if Ireland, as it moves toward Europe and the Western world, loses its spiritual and mystical centre, loses its soul, Ireland will become a strife-ridden cardboard copy of Europe and the Western world. If Ireland, as it moves toward Europe and the Western world, keeps and enhances its spiritual and mystical centre, keeps its soul, then Ireland will once more become the teacher of the western world.